GlobeTrekkerKids

VENICE TRAVEL GUIDE
FOR KID

Discovering Art, Culture, and Fun

Harper Chase

Copyright © 2024 by Harper Chase

All rights reserved. No part of this publication may be reproduced, distributed, or transmitted in any form or by any means, including photocopying, recording, or other electronic or mechanical methods, without the prior written permission of the publisher, except in the case of brief quotations embodied in critical reviews and certain other noncommercial uses permitted by copyright law.

TABLE OF CONTENTS

INTRODUCTION TO VENICE: THE FLOATING CITY 5

FINDING YOUR WAY: TIPS AND TRICKS FOR YOUNG EXPLORERS 11

VENETIAN HISTORY: TALES OF THE PAST 14

MUST-SEE SIGHTS: VENICE'S WONDERS 17

    THE GRAND CANAL 17

    ST. MARK'S BASILICA: A TREASURE TROVE OF STORIES 20

    THE DOGE'S PALACE: WHERE RULERS LIVED AND GOVERNED 23

    THE RIALTO BRIDGE 26

    THE ISLANDS OF MURANO AND BURANO: COLORS, CRAFTS, AND CHOCOLATES 29

VENETIAN CULTURE: LIVING THE ITALIAN LIFE 34

    A DAY IN THE LIFE OF A VENETIAN KID 34

    VENETIAN FESTIVALS: MASKS, COSTUMES, AND GONDOLA RACES 37

    DELICIOUS DISCOVERIES: TASTING VENICE'S CULINARY DELIGHTS 40

    VENETIAN VOCABULARY: SPEAK LIKE A LOCAL 43

    NAUTICAL TERMS FOR ASPIRING SAILORS 45

RESTAURANTS IN VENICE 48

PLANNING YOUR TRIP: TIPS FOR YOUNG TRAVELERS . 59

BEST TIMES TO VISIT VENICE WITH YOUR FAMILY .. 59
WHAT TO PACK FOR YOUR VENETIAN ADVENTURE. 63
ACCOMMODATION 66
FUN ACTIVITIES: BE AN ADVENTURER 77
FAREWELL TO VENICE 84

INTRODUCTION TO VENICE: THE FLOATING CITY

Welcome, young explorers, to one of the most magical places on Earth - Venice, Italy! Imagine a city where streets are made of water, boats replace cars, and buildings seem to float like dreams on the sea. This is Venice, the Floating City, a place unlike any other in the world.

Venice is made up of 118 small islands joined by more than 400 bridges and divided by charming canals, rather than being a single landmass.

Long ago, people built this city on wooden piles driven deep into the mud, creating a floating masterpiece that has captured adventurers' hearts for centuries.

As you flip through the pages of this guide, picture yourself gliding in a gondola through narrow waterways, under beautiful bridges, and past buildings that tell tales of a glorious past. Venice is a treasure chest of history, art, and mystery waiting to be opened.

Did you know that Venice has no cars, trucks, or buses? Instead, everyone travels by boat or on foot. This makes Venice a quiet, peaceful place, where the only sounds you might hear are the lapping of water against the sides of buildings, the distant call of a gondolier singing an Italian melody, and the laughter of children playing in the squares.

Venice is also famous for its stunning architecture and historic sites. From the dazzling St. Mark's Basilica, decorated with golden mosaics, to the grand Doge's Palace, where the rulers of Venice once lived, there is so much to see and learn.

But Venice is not just about the past. It's a living, breathing city where people live, work, and play. Venetian children go to school, play soccer in the campos (small squares), and learn to row boats just like you might ride a bicycle.

As we explore Venice together, you'll discover why this city on the water is so unique. You'll learn about its history, meet some famous (and not-so-famous) residents, and uncover hidden gems that most tourists never see.

So, grab your imaginary oar and let's set sail on an adventure through Venice, the most enchanting city on water. Who knows what secrets we'll uncover and what treasures we'll find? One thing is for sure: it will be an unforgettable journey!

Welcome aboard, young traveller, to the magical city of Venice! Let the adventure begin!

HOW VENICE WAS BUILT ON STILTS

Gather around, curious adventurers, for a tale of ingenuity, determination, and a bit of mystery! Today, we'll discover how the enchanting city of Venice was built on stilts, turning a marshy lagoon into a dazzling city on the water.

Long ago, before Venice became the floating wonder we know and love, it was just a soggy, swampy lagoon. People looking for a safe place away from invaders found this unlikely spot perfect. But there was a big challenge: How could they build a city on water?

The secret to Venice's creation lies beneath the water, hidden from view. The Venetians came up with a clever solution: they used stilts, or long wooden piles, made from alder trees. Alder wood was chosen because it's strong and, surprisingly, becomes even more complicated when submerged in water.

Imagine this: thousands upon thousands of these wooden piles were driven deep into the soft mud of the lagoon. It took great skill and hard work. Workers used boats and special tools to hammer each pile down until it reached the solid layer of clay far below the mud. This created a sturdy foundation that could support buildings, palaces, and even magnificent churches.

On top of these wooden stilts, large wooden platforms were laid to create a solid base. Then, brick and stone buildings were constructed on these platforms. It was like building a giant floating puzzle, piece by piece until a city emerged on the water.

But why didn't these wooden piles rot away? Well, that's part of the magic of Venice. The lagoon's water is low in oxygen, which helps protect the wood from decaying. Plus, the alder wood resisted the water, standing strong through the centuries. It's as if the trees knew they were part of creating something extraordinary!

Thanks to this ingenious method, Venice has stood the test of time, becoming a living masterpiece of architecture and history. It's a testament to what people can achieve when they work together and think creatively to overcome challenges.

So, next time you see a picture of Venice or, better yet, visit the floating city yourself, remember the forest of wooden stilts hidden beneath the water, holding up the city. It's a reminder that sometimes, to build something beautiful, we must think outside the box—or, in Venice's case, under the water!

And that, my young friends, is the story of how Venice was built on stilts, creating a city that seems to float like a dream on the waters of the Adriatic Sea. Isn't it amazing what wonders can be achieved with a bit of ingenuity and a lot of hard work?

NAVIGATION: EXPLORING VENICE'S WINDING CANALS

Welcome, young navigators, to the watery maze of Venice! If you've ever dreamed of being an explorer, discovering hidden paths and secret treasures, Venice is the perfect adventure for you. But before we sail on our journey, let's learn how to navigate this beautiful city of canals and islands.

Venice is like a giant puzzle, made up of many pieces—over 100 small islands, to be exact! These islands are all packed together in a narrow lagoon, linked by more than 400 bridges and separated by approximately 150 canals. Imagine that—instead of roads and highways, there are waterways where boats are the main form of transportation!

The Grand Canal is Venice's biggest and most important canal. It's like the city's main street, curving through the heart of the city in a giant S-shape. If Venice were a fish, the Grand Canal would be its spine, with all the other canals branching off like ribs. Along its banks, you'll find beautiful, old buildings that tell the story of Venice's rich history.

But how do Venetians and visitors navigate this labyrinth of waterways and narrow paths? It's all about landmarks and directions. Venetians have a unique way of giving directions, using well-known places like churches, squares (called "campos"), and bridges as reference points. Instead of saying, "Turn left or right," they might say, "Go towards San Marco, then pass by the Rialto Bridge."

Venice's maps look different from other city maps. They're filled with winding lines (the canals), tiny islands, and many little bridges. To navigate, you'll need to learn a few key names: the names of the major canals, the sestieri (the six districts of Venice), and the most important landmarks.

The sestieri are like neighbourhoods, each with its character and secrets to discover. From the bustling markets of Rialto in San Polo to the serene gardens of Castello, every area offers a new adventure. And let's remember the outer islands like Murano, known for its glassmaking, and Burano, famous for its colourful houses and lace.

Navigating Venice is part of the fun. You might get lost a few times, but that's okay! Getting lost in Venice is like opening a treasure chest full of surprises. You might stumble upon a hidden garden, a quaint little café, or a breathtaking view you'd never find in a guidebook.

So, dear explorers, remember to look around and soak in the beauty as you venture through Venice. Use your map, follow the signs, and don't be afraid to ask for directions. Every turn, every bridge, and every canal tells a story, and with a keen eye and a curious heart, you'll uncover the magic of Venice, one winding canal at a time.

Are you ready to embark on this adventure? Grab your map and sense of wonder, and let's dive into the maze of Venice's canals and islands. Who knows what amazing discoveries await us?

FINDING YOUR WAY: TIPS AND TRICKS FOR YOUNG EXPLORERS

Ahoy, young adventurers! As we set off on our journey through the enchanting city of Venice, navigating its maze of canals and alleyways might seem like a daunting task. But fear not! With a few handy tips and tricks, you'll explore Venice like a seasoned treasure hunter. Let's dive into some navigation secrets that will make your adventure fun and fruitful.

♥ Master the Map

First things first, get yourself a colourful, kid-friendly map of Venice. Look for one with big, easy-to-read landmarks and bright pictures showing the main attractions. Before you start your day, pick one or two places you'd like to visit and trace the route with your finger. This way, you'll have a mini adventure planned out in your mind.

♥ Landmarks are Your Lighthouses

In Venice, tall landmarks like the Campanile (bell tower) in St. Mark's Square can be seen from many points in the city. These landmarks are like lighthouses guiding ships to shore; they can help guide you, too! If you ever feel lost, look up and head towards a familiar landmark.

♥ The Magic of Street Signs

Venice's narrow streets are called "calli," sometimes they can be tricky to navigate. But here's a secret: look for the little signs on buildings that point towards major landmarks, like "Per San

Marco" or "Per Rialto." These signs act like breadcrumbs leading you to your destination.

♥ Bridge Names are Clues

Many of Venice's bridges have names that give you clues about what used to be there or what you'll find nearby. For example, the "Ponte delle Guglie" is adorned with spires ("guglie" in Italian). Learning a few bridge names can help you remember your routes and make for great stories, too!

♥ Ask the Locals

Don't be shy to ask for directions. Venetians are proud of their city and are usually happy to help young explorers find their way. Practice saying "Dove è...?" ("Where is...?") followed by the name of the place you're looking for. You might make a new friend and learn some interesting facts!

♥ Create a Treasure Hunt

Turn your day into a treasure hunt by making a list of things to find, like a gondola with a blue stripe, a bridge with no sides, or a shop selling gelato with more than ten flavours. This will keep your eyes peeled and your mind engaged as you navigate the city.

♥ Embrace Getting Lost

Sometimes, getting lost is the best way to discover Venice's hidden gems. You might wander into a quiet square, find a beautiful canal off the beaten path, or stumble upon a tiny bakery with the best pastries you've ever tasted. Remember, every wrong turn is an opportunity for a new adventure in Venice.

♥ Journal Your Journey

Keep a small notebook or travel journal with you to jot down the places you visit, the routes you take, and the discoveries you make along the way. You can even draw maps of your favourite spots. This will not only help you remember your journey but also turn you into a master navigator ready to tackle new adventures.

With these tips and tricks, dear explorers, you're ready to tackle Venice's winding streets and canals. Remember, every explorer needs a bit of patience, a dash of curiosity, and a big smile. So, tighten your shoelaces, grab your map, and let's set off into the heart of Venice. Who knows what unique places we'll find?

VENETIAN HISTORY: TALES OF THE PAST

Once upon a time, in a world very different from ours, there was a little group of muddy islands in the center of a shallow lagoon. This was the beginning of Venice, a place that would grow from a simple fishing village into one of history's most powerful maritime empires. Let's dive into the story of how this incredible transformation happened.

In the beginning, Venice was a refuge. People fleeing from barbarian invasions on the mainland found safety among the lagoon's difficult-to-reach islands. They were fishermen and salt workers who lived simple lives but were about to write a grand story.

As these early Venetians adapted to their watery world, they became skilled sailors and shipbuilders. They constructed sturdy boats that could navigate the lagoon's shallow waters and the open seas. Over time, Venice's strategic location turned it into a bustling trading hub. Merchants came far and wide, bringing exotic goods like spices, silk, and precious metals.

The wealth generated from trade fueled Venice's rise to power. The city became a centre of art, culture, and science, attracting thinkers, artists, and explorers. Its navy was formidable, protecting its trading routes and expanding its territories. By the Middle Ages, Venice was not just a city but a vast maritime empire; its influence was felt across the Mediterranean and beyond.

But what made Venice truly remarkable was its government. It was a republic governed by laws and led by elected officials, including the famous Doge. This system helped maintain Venice's stability and prosperity for centuries.

FAMOUS VENETIANS AND THEIR ADVENTURES

Venice was not only a powerhouse of trade and politics but also the home of some of history's most fascinating figures. Here are a couple of famous Venetians whose stories continue to inspire:

Marco Polo: Perhaps the most famous Venetian of all, Marco Polo was a merchant, traveller, and adventurer. In the late 13th century, he set off with his family on an epic journey to Asia, reaching the court of Kublai Khan in China. Through his book "The Travels of Marco Polo," Europeans were first introduced to the cultures, technologies, and wealth of the East.

Galileo Galilei: Although not born in Venice, Galileo spent significant time here and presented his famous telescope to the Venetian Senate. His discoveries—such as the moons of Jupiter—challenged how people saw the universe and laid the groundwork for modern astronomy.

Casanova: Giacomo Casanova was a writer, adventurer, and the most notorious lover in Venetian history. His autobiography reveals vivid details of 18th-century Venetian society and his escapades across Europe.

These stories of daring explorations, intellectual achievements, and thrilling adventures are just a few threads in the rich tapestry of Venetian history. They remind us that Venice was a city of merchants and sailors and a cradle of courage, imagination, and discovery.

As we sail through the pages of Venice's history, we see a city that constantly reinvented itself, navigating the waters of change with the skill of its legendary sailors. From a humble fishing village to a maritime power, Venice's story is a testament to human ingenuity, resilience, and the enduring quest for beauty and knowledge. Let's carry the spirit of Venice in our adventures, exploring the world with curiosity, bravery, and a sense of wonder.

MUST-SEE SIGHTS

MUST-SEE SIGHTS: VENICE'S WONDERS

THE GRAND CANAL

Imagine a city where the main street is not a street but a wide, sparkling river that winds through ancient buildings and under ornate bridges. Welcome to Venice and its most famous waterway, the Grand Canal!

The Grand Canal is like Venice's bustling main highway, but instead of cars and trucks, it's filled with gondolas, vaporettos (water buses), and other boats gliding gracefully through the water. This grand waterway snakes through the heart of Venice in a giant S-shape, offering a floating journey through history, beauty, and the vibrant life of this magical city.

👁 A JOURNEY ALONG THE GRAND CANAL

Starting from the lagoon near St. Mark's Square, the Grand Canal stretches over two miles through Venice, ending at the Santa Lucia train station. Along the way, it passes by palaces, churches, and old homes that tell the story of Venice's glorious past.

👁 THE PALACES OF THE GRAND CANAL

As you travel along the canal, you'll see the grand facades of Venice's most beautiful palaces. These were the homes of wealthy merchants and nobles, built to show off their riches and power. The Palazzo Venier dei Leoni, now home to the Peggy Guggenheim Collection, and the majestic Ca' d'Oro, with its ornate Gothic facade, are just two breathtaking sights.

👁 THE RIALTO BRIDGE

No journey along the Grand Canal would be complete without passing under the Rialto Bridge, one of the world's best-known and photographed bridges. It's been a busy crossing point for Venetians since the 12th century. Today, it's a bustling spot where you can find shops selling souvenirs, jewelry, and traditional Venetian crafts. The view from the bridge is one of the best in Venice, offering a panoramic vista of the city and the canal.

As you glide along the Grand Canal, the daily life of Venetians. From bustling markets and elegant cafes on the water's edge to the skilful gondoliers navigating through the crowded waterway, the Grand Canal is the lifeblood of Venice. It's a place where the past and present meet, creating a unique way of life to be seen and believed.

How to Explore the Grand Canal

The best way to experience the Grand Canal is by taking a vaporetto ride along its length. Line 1 takes you on a leisurely journey past all the major sights, allowing you to soak in the

18

beauty and grandeur of Venice from the water. For a more intimate experience, you can hire a gondola. It's more expensive, but there's nothing quite like gliding through the water in one of these elegant boats, listening to the water lap against the sides and the gondolier's oar gently stirring the canal.

The Grand Canal is not just a waterway; it's a moving stage where the drama and beauty of Venice unfold. It's a place of wonder and history, where every building tells a story, and every turn brings a new surprise. So, hop on a boat and let the Grand Canal take you on a journey through the heart of Venice. Who knows what amazing sights and stories await around the next bend?

ST. MARK'S BASILICA: A TREASURE TROVE OF STORIES

In the heart of Venice, where pigeons flutter and gondolas glide past with a whisper, stands a splendid building that seems to have been spun from gold and dreams. This is St. Mark's Basilica, a dazzling jewel in the crown of Venice, brimming with stories waiting to be told. Let's open the book on this magnificent treasure trove of history, art, and mystery.

👁 A BASILICA BORN FROM ADVENTURE

Our story begins with a daring adventure, much like the ones you dream of embarking on. Imagine, long ago, two Venetian merchants setting off across the sea. Their mission? To bring back the relics of St. Mark the Evangelist from faraway lands. Despite facing many dangers, they succeeded, and the people of Venice decided to build a magnificent church to house these sacred treasures. This church, dedicated to St. Mark, would become the heart and soul of Venice.

👁 A MOSAIC OF STORIES

As you step inside St. Mark's Basilica, your eyes will be met by a shimmering spectacle. The ceilings and walls are covered in mosaics that tell stories from the Bible, sparkling with gold, green, blue, and every colour imaginable. These are not just decorations but books written in glass and gold, telling tales of faith, courage, and the saints who walked before us. Each piece of glass, each fragment of stone, was placed by hand, creating a masterpiece that took centuries to complete.

👁 THE PALA D'ORO

Hidden within St. Mark's Basilica is one of its most precious treasures, the Pala d'Oro, a gold altarpiece adorned with hundreds of precious gems. It's like something out of a fairy tale, glinting with rubies, sapphires, emeralds, and pearls. This masterpiece tells its own story of devotion, craftsmanship, and the Venetians' love for their city and its patron saint.

👁 THE FOUR HORSES

Above the great doors of the basilica stand four bronze horses, their muscles tensed, ready to leap into the sky. These horses have their own incredible journey, having travelled from ancient Constantinople to Venice as spoils of war. They are symbols of Venice's power and glory and the city's connection to the wider world, a reminder of the days when Venetian ships sailed to distant lands.

👁 A SYMPHONY IN STONE

St. Mark's Basilica is more than just a church; it's a symphony in stone and mosaic, where every column, every statue, and every carving has its part to play. The basilica's design blends the East and West, reflecting Venice's role as a bridge between cultures. It's a place where you can feel the whispers of history, where every corner holds a secret waiting to be discovered.

Exploring St. Mark's Basilica is like embarking on a treasure hunt, where every step brings you face-to-face with wonders from a bygone era. You'll wander in awe under the golden domes, past marble columns that have stood for centuries, and through quiet chapels filled with the scent of incense and history.

So, young adventurers, are you ready to explore St. Mark's Basilica? Remember, as you walk through its grand doors, you're stepping into a story that stretches back through time. Look closely, listen carefully, and let the basilica reveal its tales of adventure, beauty, and faith. Who knows what stories you'll discover hidden within its ancient walls?

THE DOGE'S PALACE: WHERE RULERS LIVED AND GOVERNED

In the heart of Venice, beside the shimmering waters and the bustling St. Mark's Square, stands a grand and mysterious building that whispers tales of power, intrigue, and luxury. This is the Doge's Palace, where Venice's rulers, known as Doges, lived and governed the city for over a thousand years. Let's journey through time to explore this magnificent palace, unlocking secrets and stories from Venice's golden past.

👁 A PALACE OF POWER AND BEAUTY

The Doge's Palace, with its intricate façade of white limestone and pink marble, looks like a masterpiece painted against the sky. Its delicate arches and ornate balconies might make you think it's a palace of fairy tales, yet it was here that the Doge and Venice's government made decisions that would shape the destiny of this maritime Republic.

👁 THE HALLS OF POWER

Stepping inside the Doge's Palace is like entering a world where every wall, ceiling, and corner tells a story. The grand halls are adorned with paintings and frescoes by some of Venice's greatest artists, including Tintoretto and Veronese. These aren't just decorations; they are messages of power, justice, and the glory of the Republic of Venice.

One of the most awe-inspiring rooms is the Great Council Hall, one of the largest rooms in Europe. It was here that the Great Council, comprising hundreds of members of Venice's noble families, gathered to decide on matters of state. Imagine the echoes of debates, the rustle of luxurious robes, and the weight of decisions that shaped the course of history, all within these walls.

👁 THE BRIDGE OF SIGHS

One of the most famous parts of the Doge's Palace isn't a room but a bridge. The Bridge of Sighs, a covered passageway made of white limestone with windows barred by stone, connects the palace to the prisons. It is said that prisoners would sigh at their final view of beautiful Venice through the window before being taken to their cells. The bridge is a reminder of the Republic's strict governance, where justice was swift, and mercy was rare.

👁 THE SECRET ITINERARIES

The Doge's Palace holds mysteries and hidden corners that tell the darker side of Venice's history. Secret itineraries lead through narrow corridors and hidden rooms where the city's secret service operated, spying on citizens and ensuring the Doge's power remained unchallenged. These secret passages reveal the complexity of Venetian politics and the lengths to which the rulers would go to maintain control.

👁 A LIVING LEGACY

Today, the Doge's Palace is a testament to Venice's grandeur and complex political history. It's a place where you can walk in the footsteps of rulers, soldiers, and prisoners and feel the weight of history in its halls.

Young explorers, as you wander through the Doge's Palace, let your imagination run wild. Picture the Doges in their regal robes, the bustling of government officials through the corridors, and the silent whispers of secrets passed in hidden rooms. The Doge's Palace is not just a building; it's a portal to the past, inviting you to uncover the stories and secrets that have shaped Venice into the enchanting city it is today.

THE RIALTO BRIDGE

In the magical city of Venice, where the streets are made of water and boats are the favourite way to travel, there stands a bridge famous not just for its stunning architecture but also for the bustling market that has thrived on its steps for centuries. The most ancient bridge on the Grand Canal, the Rialto Bridge serves as the hub of daily activity and commerce in Venice. Let's take a stroll across this remarkable bridge and discover the treasures it holds.

👁 A BRIDGE FULL OF HISTORY

With its distinctive design and excellent location, the Rialto Bridge has been a focal point of Venice since it was first built as a pontoon bridge in the 12th century. The version we see today, made of stone with its distinctive arch, was completed in 1591. It was an architectural marvel of its time, designed to allow ships to pass beneath and to support the weight of the shops built into its structure.

👁 A MARKETPLACE LIKE NO OTHER

Imagine a place where the air is filled with the chatter of shopkeepers, the scent of fresh produce, and the vibrant colours of handcrafted goods. This is the Rialto Market, located at the foot of the Rialto Bridge. For hundreds of years, Venetians and visitors have flocked to this market to buy the freshest fish, vegetables, fruits, and spices. Every stall tells a story, and every shopkeeper knows the secret to the perfect Venetian dish.

👁 SHOPPING ON THE BRIDGE

The Rialto Bridge is home to various shops, making it the perfect place for a shopping adventure. As you walk across the bridge, you'll find small boutiques nestled within its arches, selling everything from exquisite Murano glass jewelry to handmade Venetian masks that seem to whisper tales of mystery and intrigue. Each shop is a treasure trove of local craftsmanship, offering unique souvenirs and gifts you won't find anywhere else.

👁 THE HEARTBEAT OF VENICE

The Rialto Bridge is more than simply a shopping destination; it's where you can feel the pulse of Venice. Standing in the centre of the bridge, you can watch gondolas and vaporettos gliding along the Grand Canal, and the panoramic view of the city's rooftops and bell towers is breathtaking. It's a spot where you can pause and realize you're standing in the heart of one of the most beautiful cities on earth.

Every corner of the Rialto Bridge and its market is filled with stories. From the fishmongers who rise before dawn to bring you the catch of the day to the artisans who craft beautiful works of art, everyone has a tale to share. The bridge is a living museum where history, culture, and daily life come together in a vibrant display of Venetian spirit.

So, dear young explorers, next time you find yourself wandering across the Rialto Bridge, take a moment to listen to the stories being told. Dive into the bustling market, peek into the shops, and let the bridge's stones whisper to you the tales of centuries past. The Rialto Bridge isn't just a crossing over water; it's a journey through the heart of Venice, offering endless discoveries and treasures waiting to be found.

THE ISLANDS OF MURANO AND BURANO: COLORS, CRAFTS, AND CHOCOLATES

Just a short boat journey from Venice's bustling streets lies two magnificent islands, each with its charm and secrets waiting to be revealed. Welcome to Murano and Burano, where colours dance, crafts tell stories and even chocolates can taste like adventures. Let's sail to these enchanting islands and uncover their wonders.

👁 MURANO: THE ISLAND OF GLASS

As your boat approaches Murano, you'll first notice the shimmering reflections of sunlight bouncing off the colourful facades of the buildings. But Murano's true magic lies in its ancient craft of glassmaking. For centuries, the world's finest glassblowers have called this island home, creating everything from delicate vases to whimsical sculptures, all with a breath of air and a twist of skill.

👁 A VISIT TO THE GLASS FURNACES

Imagine stepping into a workshop where fire roars and molten glass glows like liquid jewels. Here, you can watch master craftsmen, known as "maestri," transform this fiery liquid into stunning artwork right before your eyes. The air is warm, the light flickers and the atmosphere is filled with the magic of creation.

👁 THE GLASS MUSEUM

For those curious about the history and artistry behind Murano glass, the Glass Museum is a treasure trove of sparkling wonders. It's like walking through a rainbow made solid, with centuries of glassmaking history on display, showcasing how this art has evolved while keeping its magic alive.

30

👁 BURANO

Leaving Murano's fiery furnaces behind, our next stop is Burano, an island painted in a palette of dreams. Each house is a splash of colour, from sunny yellows to vibrant blues, creating a kaleidoscope of hues that seem to dance under the Italian sun.

👁 THE LACE MAKERS OF BURANO

Burano is famed not just for their colours but also for its exquisite lace. This delicate craft has been passed down through generations, with needle lace being the island's speciality. Watching the lace makers at work is like witnessing a ballet of fingers as intricate patterns come to life, stitch by stitch.

👁 A SWEET SURPRISE

And what's a visit to Burano without a taste of its sweetest delight? The island is known for its "bussolà," a traditional buttery biscuit that melts in your mouth. Some say it tastes like happiness, shaped into a ring of golden goodness.

👁 THE CHOCOLATE ADVENTURE

While Venice and its islands are not traditionally known for chocolate, let's imagine a sweet twist in our tale. Picture a small, hidden shop in Burano, where a chocolatier crafts chocolates that capture the essence of these islands. Each piece is a bite of beauty, with flavours inspired by Burano's colours and Murano glass's sparkle. It's a place where even chocolate tells a story.

Murano and Burano are more than just islands near Venice; they are worlds unto themselves, brimming with artistry, history, and colour. They remind us that beauty can be crafted from fire, that the world is a canvas of colours waiting to be appreciated, and that sometimes, the sweetest adventures come in the most unexpected forms.

So, dear young explorers, let the islands of Murano and Burano remind us to seek beauty in the world, cherish the crafts and stories of those who came before us, and always keep an eye out for the magic hidden in everyday moments. Who knows what wonders you'll discover on your own adventures?

VENETIAN CULTURE

VENETIAN CULTURE: LIVING THE ITALIAN LIFE

A DAY IN THE LIFE OF A VENETIAN KID

Life flows at a unique pace in the wonderful city of Venice, where canals replace streets and boats are the primary way to get around. Let's dive into a day in the life of a Venetian kid, where every moment is an adventure waiting to happen, surrounded by history, culture, and the vibrant spirit of Italy.

♥ MORNING: SCHOOL AND SCENIC COMMUTES

The day starts with the sun rising over the lagoon, painting the sky in shades of pink and orange. For a Venetian kid, it's time to get ready for school. But there's no school bus waiting; instead, there's a vaporetto, the water bus, making its way through the canals. Imagine stepping onto the boat, greeting friends, and watching the historic buildings glide by as you make your way to school. It's a commute like no other, filled with the beauty of Venice at every turn.

♥ AFTER SCHOOL: PLAYTIME IN PIAZZAS

Once the school day ends, the real fun begins. Venetian kids don't head to typical playgrounds; instead, they play in the campos, the small squares dotted around the city. These open spaces are where local kids gather to play soccer, tag, chat, and enjoy gelato. The sound of laughter and chatter fills the air, blending with the gentle splash of nearby canals.

♥ HOMEWORK WITH A VIEW

Homework might not be the most exciting part of the day, but in Venice, even homework comes with a view. Picture sitting at a desk, your window open to a canal below, where gondolas and boats pass by, serenaded by the distant melody of a singing gondolier. It's a backdrop that turns even the most mundane tasks into magic moments.

♥ EVENING: FAMILY TIME

Dinner time is family time in Venice, as in all of Italy. Families congregate to eat together at the table, often featuring fresh seafood from the lagoon, homemade pasta, and a delicious tiramisu for dessert. It's a time for stories, laughter, and the warmth of family. After dinner, a passeggiata, or evening stroll, is a common tradition. Walking through the winding streets and over bridges, Venetian kids enjoy the cooler air and the beautifully lit pathways, saying hello to neighbours and stopping to admire the nighttime reflections in the water.

♥ WEEKENDS: ADVENTURES AWAIT

On weekends, the whole city becomes a playground. There might be a visit to the Rialto Market to help choose fresh ingredients for the week's meals, a boat trip to the nearby islands of Murano or Burano, or a family outing to one of Venice's many festivals. Each weekend brings a new adventure, an opportunity to explore and discover the wonders of Venice and its rich culture.

♥ LIVING THE VENETIAN DREAM

For a kid in Venice, life is intertwined with the city's history, beauty, and unique way of life. Every day is a chance to explore ancient palazzos, learn the stories of the past, and make memories that will last a lifetime. It's a life where the ordinary becomes extraordinary, set against the backdrop of one of the world's most beautiful cities.

Dear young readers, imagine yourself in the shoes of a Venetian kid, living a life filled with adventure, history, and the joy of Italian culture. Venice is not just a place; it's a way of life where every day is a journey through a living museum, and every moment is a chance to discover something new.

VENETIAN FESTIVALS: MASKS, COSTUMES, AND GONDOLA RACES

In the wonderful city of Venice, where the streets are made of water and the air is filled with history, the calendar is dotted with festivals that light up the city with colour, excitement, and tradition. Let's get into the heart of Venetian culture and discover the magic of its festivals, where masks, costumes, and gondola races bring the city to life.

♥ CARNEVALE: A MASKED MARVEL

Imagine a time when the streets of Venice become a stage, and everyone is a character in a grand, mysterious play. This is Carnevale, Venice's most famous festival, taking place in the weeks leading up to Lent. The city bursts into a kaleidoscope of colours, with people wearing elaborate masks and costumes that range from beautiful to bizarre. The masks are not just for fun; they were traditionally used to hide the wearer's identity, allowing everyone, from dukes to commoners, to mix in celebration.

♥ THE FLIGHT OF THE ANGEL

One of the highlights of Carnevale is the "Flight of the Angel," where an acrobat or a special guest descends from the Campanile (bell tower) in St. Mark's Square, gliding down to the crowd below on a rope. It's a breathtaking spectacle that combines bravery, beauty, and the thrill of the unexpected.

♥ FESTA DEL REDENTORE: FIREWORKS AND FEASTS

As summer warms the canals, Venice celebrates the Festa del Redentore, commemorating the end of a terrible plague in the 16th century. The festival is known for its stunning fireworks display over the lagoon, creating reflections in the water that rival the beauty of the stars above. Families and friends gather on boats, rooftops, and along the canals to share meals and watch the sky light up in a dazzling display of colours and patterns.

♥ REGATA STORICA: A RACE THROUGH HISTORY

The first Sunday of September brings the Regata Storica, Venice's historic boat race. This event is not just a test of skill and speed but a journey through time, as rowers dress in traditional costumes and compete in boats used in Venice for centuries. The race is preceded by a dramatic procession of ancient ships, complete with gondoliers dressed in period costumes, commemorating Venice's extensive nautical heritage.

♥ THE THRILL OF THE RACE

The heart of the Regata Storica is the competition, where teams in different categories race along the Grand Canal, cheered on by crowds of locals and visitors alike. The most anticipated race involves the gondolini, slim, fast gondolas rowed by the city's best oarsmen. It's a thrilling sight as the boats slice through the water, oars flashing, in a battle of strength, strategy, and tradition.

♥ LA FESTA DELLA SENSA: MARRIAGE TO THE SEA

Another unique Venetian festival is La Festa della Sensa, celebrating Venice's historic relationship with the sea. This ancient ceremony symbolizes the marriage between Venice and the sea, with the city's mayor throwing a ring into the lagoon to affirm Venice's dominion over the waters. It's a beautiful blend of pageantry, spirituality, and community, highlighting Venetians' deep connection with their aquatic environment.

♥ LIVING THE FESTIVE SPIRIT

Venetian festivals are more than just events; they are a vibrant expression of the city's soul, blending history, art, and community in a tapestry of traditions that continue to enchant and inspire. For those lucky enough to experience these festivals, they offer a chance to step into a world of wonder, where the past and present dance together in the streets and canals of Venice.

Dear young adventurers, let the spirit of Venice's festivals ignite your imagination. Remember: in this city of masks, costumes, and gondola races, every day is an invitation to celebrate the beauty and mystery of life.

DELICIOUS DISCOVERIES: TASTING VENICE'S CULINARY DELIGHTS

Welcome, young food explorers, to a tasty adventure through the enchanting city of Venice! Here, every winding canal and cobblestone street leads to delicious discoveries and culinary treats as unique as the city. Let's embark on a gastronomic journey to taste the flavours of Venice, where each dish tells a story of history, tradition, and the magic of Italian cooking.

♥ CICCHETTI: VENICE'S ANSWER TO TAPAS

Our first stop is a cosy bacaro, a traditional Venetian bar, where locals gather to enjoy cicchetti (pronounced chee-KET-tee), small snacks or side dishes that are Venice's answer to tapas. Imagine plates filled with tiny sandwiches, seafood on crostini, and fried olives; all meant to be shared. Each cicchetto is a bite-sized glimpse into the flavours of Venice, perfect for tasting a little bit of everything.

40

♥ RISOTTO AL NERO DI SEPPIA: A BOLD FLAVOR

Next on our culinary adventure is risotto al nero di seppia, a striking black risotto colored with cuttlefish ink.

This dish combines creamy rice with the rich, briny flavor of the sea, creating a taste that's as bold and mysterious as Venice itself. It's a dish that might make you think of pirates and hidden treasures with its dark colour and deep flavour.

♥ SARDE IN SAOR: A SWEET AND SOUR DELIGHT

Sarde in saor is a dish that takes you back in time. It's a recipe born from the need to preserve food on long sea voyages. It's made with fried sardines marinated in a sweet and sour mixture of onions, vinegar, raisins, and pine nuts. The result is a delightful harmony of flavours that speaks to Venice's history as a maritime power and its connection to distant lands and spices.

♥ GELATO: A CREAMY DREAM

No culinary exploration is complete without dessert, and in Venice, that means gelato! Strolling through the streets with a cone of creamy, dreamy gelato in hand is a joy. From basic flavours like chocolate and strawberry to more daring ones like tiramisu and pistachio, each scoop tastes Italian sweetness that will make your heart sing.

♥ FRITTELLE: CARNIVAL TREATS

If you're lucky enough to visit Venice during Carnevale, you'll find the air filled with the sweet scent of frittelle, soft, fried doughnuts that are a seasonal treat. These fluffy balls of joy can be plain, filled with cream, or studded with raisins and pine nuts. Biting into a warm frittella is like tasting a piece of Venice's festive spirit.

Eating your way through Venice is like going on a treasure hunt, where each dish leads you to new discoveries about the city's culture, history, and way of life. From the bustling Rialto Market with its fresh produce and seafood to the quiet cafes by the canals where you can savour a slice of tiramisu, Venice offers a feast for the senses.

As you explore Venice, remember to savour each bite, taste each flavour, and let the city's culinary delights guide you on an unforgettable journey of discovery. Venice isn't just a feast for the eyes; it's a banquet for the taste buds, inviting you to explore, taste, and fall in love with its delicious wonders.

VENETIAN VOCABULARY: SPEAK LIKE A LOCAL

Welcome to Venice, a city of waterways, wonder, and words! To truly immerse yourself in the Venetian way of life, it helps to know a few local phrases. Speaking like a local opens doors to hidden gems and weaves you into this magical city's fabric of daily life. Let's dive into some handy phrases for your everyday adventures in Venice.

GREETINGS AND POLITE EXPRESSIONS

- Buongiorno! (**bwon-JOR-no**) - Good morning! It is a cheerful way to greet everyone you meet, from the Vaporetto driver to the shopkeeper.
- Buonasera! (**bwon-a-SER-a**) - Good evening! As the day turns into night, switch your greeting to match the time of day.
- Per favore (**per fa-VO-re**) - Please. Adding this to any request makes it sweeter.
- Grazie! (**GRA-tsie**) - Thank you! Always remember to show your appreciation.
- Scusi (**SKOO-zi**)—Excuse me. This is a must-know word whether you're navigating through crowded streets or asking for directions.
- Dove è...? (**DO-ve eh...?**) - Where is...? Follow this with the place you're looking for, and you're on your way to discovering Venice's secrets.

FOOD AND DINING

- Posso avere...? (**PO-so a-VE-re...?**) - May I have...? Use this phrase when ordering your gelato or a slice of pizza.

- Un gelato, per favore! (**OON je-LA-to, per fa-VO-re**) - A gelato, please! Because no day is complete without a scoop of Italian ice cream.
- L'acqua (**L'AK-kwa**) - Water. Staying hydrated is vital while exploring.
- Il conto, per favore (**il KON-to, per fa-VO-re**) - The bill, please. When you're ready to leave a café or restaurant.

GETTING AROUND

- Dove posso trovare...? (**DO-ve POS-so tro-VA-re...?**) - Where can I find...? It is essential for locating anything from the nearest bathroom to a hidden museum.
- Quanto costa? (**KWAN-to KO-sta?**) - How much does it cost? Always good to know before you hop on a gondola ride or purchase souvenirs.
- La fermata del vaporetto (**la fer-MA-ta del va-po-RET-to**) - The vaporetto stop. The water buses are your best friends for getting around Venice.

MAKING FRIENDS

- Come ti chiami? (**KO-me ti KYA-mi?**) - What's your name? A great way to start a conversation with a fellow young explorer.
- Mi chiamo... (**mi KYA-mo...**) - My name is... Share a bit about yourself and make new friends along the way.
- Che bello! (**ke BEL-lo!**) - How beautiful! Whether you're admiring a sunset over the Grand Canal or a piece of Venetian glass, this phrase expresses your appreciation.

Learning these phrases is like finding the key to a secret garden, unlocking a richer, more authentic experience in Venice. Don't worry about making mistakes; the locals will appreciate your effort to speak their language. So, take a deep breath, let your curiosity lead the way, and remember, every word is a step on your Venetian adventure. Buona fortuna, and enjoy the magic of Venice!

NAUTICAL TERMS FOR ASPIRING SAILORS

Ahoy, young adventurers! Are you ready to set sail on the high seas of knowledge and learn the language of sailors? Every sailor, from the seasoned captain to the eager deckhand, speaks a unique language that helps them navigate the waters, control their ship, and embark on maritime adventures. Let's dive into the world of nautical terms, and soon, you'll be talking like a true sailor!

SHIP PARTS AND PLACES

- **BOW** (Pronounced like 'wow') - The front part of the ship. It's the first part to meet the waves!
- **STERN** - The back part of the ship. It's where you can stand and wave goodbye to the shore as you embark on your voyage.
- **PORT:** The left side of the ship when you're facing the bow. Remember, "port" and "left" both have four letters!
- **STARBOARD:** The right side of the ship when you're facing the bow. It's the side that used to be used for steering before ships had rudders.

- **DECK:** The outside top part of the ship where you can walk around and enjoy the sea breeze.
- **MAST:** The tall vertical pole(s) that hold up the sails. They're like the trees of the ship, reaching up to catch the wind.

SAILING AND MANEUVERING

- **HOIST** - To raise something, like a sail or a flag, up the mast. It's like saying, "Up you go!"
- **TACK** - To turn the bow of the ship through the wind so that the wind changes from one side of the ship to the other. It's a nifty maneuver to help change direction.
- **JIBE (OR GYBE)** - To turn the stern through the wind, making the wind switch sides across the back of the ship. It's the opposite of tacking and requires a bit of skill!
- **ANCHOR**—not just a term but a crucial tool. To anchor, drop the anchor into the water to hold the ship in place. It's like putting the ship's parking brake on.

WIND AND WEATHER

- **BREEZE:** A light wind that makes for perfect sailing conditions. It's the sea's way of giving you a gentle push.
- **GALE -** A very strong wind. When sailors talk about a gale, they're preparing for a stormy challenge.
- **KNOT** - A measure of speed on the water. One knot is equivalent to a nautical mile per hour. It's how sailors know how fast they're going without a speedometer.

SAILOR SPEAK

- **AHOY** - A way to greet someone or get their attention. It's the "hello" of the high seas.
- **MATEY** - A friend or companion. Your fellow sailors are your mateys when you're part of a crew.
- **AVAST** - A command to stop or pay attention. It's like saying, "Hey, look at this!" or "Stop what you're doing!"

Learning these nautical terms is your first step into the vast world of sailing and the sea. With these words in your sailor's toolkit, you're ready to embark on imaginary voyages across the globe, navigate the storied waters of ancient mariners, and dream of your own maritime adventures. So, raise the anchor, hoist the sails, and set course for adventure on the high seas. Who knows what wonders you'll discover with the wind in your sails and a sea of knowledge at your helm?

RESTAURANTS IN VENICE
♥ IMPRONTA
♦ Sestiere Dorsoduro 3815, 30123 Venice Italy
☏ +39 041 275 0386

Hours

Mon

7:00 AM - 12:00 AM

Tue

7:00 AM - 12:00 AM

Wed

7:00 AM - 12:00 AM

Thu

7:00 AM - 12:00 AM

Fri

7:00 AM - 12:00 AM

Sat

8:00 AM - 12:00 AM

PRICE RANGE

$43 – $96

CUISINES

Italian, Seafood, Mediterranean, European, Healthy

SPECIAL DIETS

Vegetarian Friendly, Vegan Options, Gluten Free Options

MEALS

Lunch, Dinner, Brunch

FEATURES

Reservations, Seating, Highchairs Available, Wheelchair Accessible, Serves Alcohol, Full Bar, Wine and Beer, Accepts American Express, Accepts Mastercard, Accepts Visa, Digital Payments, Free Wifi, Accepts Credit Cards, Table Service, Dog Friendly, Non-smoking restaurants.

♥ LA CARAVELLA

- via XXII Marzo 2399 San Marco, 30124 Venice Italy
- +39 041 520 8901

Hours

Sunday

12:00 PM - 3:30 PM

7:00 PM - 11:00 PM

Mon

12:00 PM - 3:30 PM

7:00 PM - 11:00 PM

Tue

12:00 PM - 3:30 PM

7:00 PM - 11:00 PM

Wed

12:00 PM - 3:30 PM

7:00 PM - 11:00 PM

Thu

12:00 PM - 3:30 PM

7:00 PM - 11:00 PM

Fri

12:00 PM - 3:30 PM

7:00 PM - 11:00 PM

Sat

12:00 PM - 3:30 PM

7:00 PM - 11:00 PM

PRICE RANGE

$53 – $160

CUISINES

Italian, Seafood, Mediterranean, European

SPECIAL DIETS

Vegetarian Friendly, Vegan Options, Gluten Free Options

MEALS

Lunch, Dinner

FEATURES

Reservations, Outdoor Seating, Seating, Highchairs Available, Wheelchair Accessible, Serves Alcohol, Full Bar, Accepts American Express, Accepts Mastercard, Accepts Visa, Digital Payments, Free Wifi, Accepts Credit Cards, Table Service, Gift Cards Available.

♥ AL GRILL

- Santa Croce 2097, 30135 Venice Italy
- +39 041 319 4621

IN ORDER TO TAKE ONE MUST GIVE.
POUR RECEVOIR, IL FAUT DONNER.
WER NIMMT, MUSS AUCH GEBEN.

Hours

Sun

12:00 PM - 11:00 PM

Mon

12:00 PM - 11:00 PM

Wed

12:00 PM - 11:00 PM

Thu

12:00 PM - 11:00 PM

Fri

12:00 PM - 11:00 PM

Sat

12:00 PM - 11:00 PM

CUISINES

Italian, Steakhouse, Barbecue, Grill

MEALS

Lunch, Dinner

FEATURES

Reservations, Seating, Serves Alcohol, Full Bar, Table Service

♥ EL FRADEO QUEBRADO

- Campo S. Giacomo Dall'Orio Santa Croce, 1464, 30135 Venice Italy
- +39 345 619 7737

Hours

Sun

10:00 AM - 11:00 PM

Mon

10:00 AM - 11:00 PM

Tue

10:00 AM - 11:00 PM

Wed

10:00 AM - 11:00 PM

Thu

10:00 AM - 11:00 PM

Fri

10:00 AM - 11:00 PM

Sat

10:00 AM - 11:00 PM

MEALS

Drinks

♥ VINERIA ALL'AMARONE
- C. dei Sbianchesini, 1131, 30125 Venice Italy
- +39 041 523 1184

Hours

Tue	12:00 PM - 10:30 PM
12:00 PM - 10:30 PM	Fri
Wed	12:00 PM - 10:30 PM
12:00 PM - 10:30 PM	Sat
Thu	12:00 PM - 10:30 PM

PRICE RANGE

$85 – $149

CUISINES

Italian, Mediterranean, European, Wine Bar

MEALS

Lunch, Dinner, Drinks

FEATURES

Outdoor Seating, Seating, Wheelchair Accessible, Serves Alcohol, Full Bar, Wine and Beer, Accepts American Express, Accepts Mastercard, Accepts Visa, Digital Payments, Free Wifi, Accepts Credit Cards, Table Service, Non-smoking restaurants, Gift Cards Available

♥ ALL'ARCO
- Calle Dell'occhialer 436, 30125 Venice Italy
- +39 041 520 5666

Hours

Sun	Thu
10:00 am - 2:30 pm	10:00 am - 2:30 pm
Mon	Fri
10:00 am - 2:30 pm	10:00 am - 2:30 pm
Tue	Sat
10:00 am - 2:30 pm	10:00 am - 2:30 pm

CUISINES

Italian, Wine Bar

SPECIAL DIETS

Vegetarian Friendly

MEALS

Lunch, Drinks

FEATURES

Takeout, Outdoor Seating, Wheelchair Accessible, Serves Alcohol

PLANNING YOUR TRIP: TIPS FOR YOUNG TRAVELERS

BEST TIMES TO VISIT VENICE WITH YOUR FAMILY

Venice, with its winding canals, historic bridges, and magical squares, has sprung from the pages of a fairy tale. Planning a journey to this wonderful city with your family is an adventure, and deciding when to visit can make all the difference. Let's journey through the seasons to discover the perfect time for young travellers and their families to explore Venice.

SPRING: BLOOMING WITH BEAUTY

As the chill of winter melts away, Venice awakens in the spring with warmer weather and blooming flowers. From March to May, the city is less crowded, allowing you and your family to wander through its alleys and over its bridges more freely. The temperatures are mild, perfect for exploring outdoor attractions like St. Mark's Square, the Doge's Palace, and the Rialto Bridge without getting too hot or cold.

Why Spring?

- **Fewer Crowds:** Before the summer rush, you'll have more space to explore.
- **Gentle Weather:** Enjoy outdoor adventures without the summer heat.
- **Vibrant Life:** Watch Venice come to life with spring and Easter celebrations.

SUMMER: A FESTIVE AND SUNNY SEASON

From June to August, Venice shines with sunlight and festivities in summer. This is the high season, full of energy and excitement, with tourists from around the globe. While it can be pretty warm and crowded, the summer also brings long days perfect for adventure and nights filled with cultural events.

Why Summer?

- **Festivals Galore:** Experience the Festa del Redentore with its spectacular fireworks.
- **Open Attractions:** With longer hours for museums and other attractions, there's more time to explore.
- **Vibrant Atmosphere:** The city buzzes with outdoor dining, street performers, and lively markets.

AUTUMN

September to November in Venice is a time of mellow beauty and fewer tourists. The crisp, chilly air of autumn replaces the heat of summer, making it a great time for families to take long walks and appreciate the city's outdoor beauty. The shifting leaves and softer light add charm to the already breathtaking surroundings.

Why Autumn?

- **Mild Weather:** Comfortable temperatures make exploring a breeze.
- **Less Crowded:** With the summer crowds gone, Venice feels more relaxed.
- **Cultural Events:** Autumn brings film festivals and the historical Regata Storica boat race.

WINTER: QUIET CHARM AND CARNIVAL

Winter, from December to February, transforms Venice into a serene, misty wonderland. This is the quietest time in Venice, offering a more intimate experience of the city's charm. If you visit in February, you might also catch the Carnevale, a world-famous festival where Venice is at its most vibrant, filled with masks, costumes, and revelry.

Why Winter?

- **Carnevale:** Experience the magic of Venice's famous carnival.

- **Peaceful Exploration:** Enjoy the city without the crowds at a more leisurely pace.
- **Winter Beauty:** See a different side of Venice, with misty mornings and quiet canals.

TIPS FOR YOUNG TRAVELERS

- **Pack for the Weather:** Whether sun hats and sunscreen for summer or warm coats and boots for winter, being prepared will make your trip more comfortable.
- **Stay Flexible:** Venice is a city of surprises. Be ready to explore hidden alleys, discover unexpected sights, and enjoy the adventure.
- **Learn Together:** Before your trip, explore books and stories about Venice. Learning about the city's history and culture can make your visit even more exciting.

Choosing the best time to visit Venice with your family depends on what you're looking for in your adventure. Whether you seek the lively buzz of summer festivals, the serene beauty of winter, the fresh bloom of spring, or the crisp autumn air, Venice welcomes you with open arms and countless wonders. So pack your bags, grab your family, and get ready for an unforgettable journey to the heart of this timeless city.

WHAT TO PACK FOR YOUR VENETIAN ADVENTURE

Embarking on a journey to Venice, the city of canals and dreams, is an adventure. Whether you're navigating its winding waterways, exploring its ancient alleyways, or marvelling at its majestic buildings, having the right items in your suitcase can make your Venetian adventure even more magical. So, let's dive into the essentials you'll need to pack for a trip to this enchanting city.

CLOTHING FOR ALL SEASONS

- **Comfortable Walking Shoes:** Venice is best explored on foot, so wear strong and comfortable shoes for all of your walking and exploration.
- **Layered Clothing:** The weather in Venice can change quickly, no matter the season. Pack layers that can be quickly added and removed, such as t-shirts, sweaters, and a lightweight, waterproof jacket.
- **Sun Protection:** During the warmer months, remember to bring sunglasses, a hat, and sunscreen to protect yourself from the sun while you walk through the city's open squares and canals.

ADVENTURE GEAR

- **Waterproof Bag:** Venice is surrounded by water, and sometimes, especially during high tide (acqua alta), you might find yourself navigating through wet streets. Your stuff will stay dry and safe if you use a waterproof bag.
- **Portable Water Bottle:** Staying hydrated during your adventures is vital. Bring a reusable water bottle; there are

many public fountains around Venice where you can refill it with fresh, clean water.

CULTURAL EXPLORATION KIT

- **Notebook and Pen:** Venice will inspire you with its beauty and history. Bring a notebook and pen to jot down your ideas, sketch the surroundings, or keep a travel journal about your adventures.
- **Camera or Smartphone:** You'll want to capture the memories of your Venetian adventure, from the grandeur of St. Mark's Basilica to the colourful houses of Burano. Make sure you have a camera or smartphone with plenty of storage space.
- **Italian Phrasebook:** Knowing a few key phrases in Italian can enrich your experience. A phrasebook or a language app can help you communicate with locals and immerse yourself in Venetian culture.

EXTRAS FOR FAMILY FUN

- **Travel Games and Books:** For downtime or relaxing evenings, pack a few travel games, cards, or books that the whole family can enjoy together.
- **Snacks:** Exploring can work up an appetite. Pack non-perishable snacks like nuts, granola bars, or crackers for a quick energy boost.
- **Disposable Rain Ponchos:** Quick and easy to pack, disposable rain ponchos can be a lifesaver during

unexpected showers, ensuring the weather doesn't dampen your spirits.

Remember, keeping it simple and versatile is the key to packing for Venice. Venice is a city of art, history, and mystery waiting to be explored. With these essentials in your suitcase, you're ready to embark on your Venetian adventure, creating memories that will last a lifetime. So pack your bags, adventurers, and get ready to be enchanted by the wonders of Venice!

ACCOMMODATION

KIDS FRIENDLY HOTELS IN VENICE

♥ HOTEL MORESCO

- Sestiere Dorsoduro 3499, 30123 Venice Italy
- 009 39 041 244 0202

Property amenities

- Free High Speed Internet (WiFi)
- Free breakfast
- Airport Transportation
- 24-hour security
- Baggage storage

- 24-hour front desk
- Private check-in / check-out
- Dry cleaning
- Wifi
- Bar / lounge
- Breakfast buffet
- Breakfast in the room
- Complimentary Instant Coffee
- Special diet menus
- Wine / champagne
- Car hire
- Taxi service
- Concierge
- Newspaper
- Shared lounge / TV area
- Laundry service
- Ironing service

Room features

- Soundproof rooms
- Bathrobes
- Air conditioning
- Desk
- Housekeeping
- Minibar
- Flatscreen TV
- Bath / shower
- Safe
- Telephone
- Wake-up service / alarm clock
- Refrigerator
- Complimentary toiletries
- Hair dryer

Room types

- Non-smoking rooms
- Suites

LANGUAGES SPOKEN

- English
- French
- Spanish
- Croatian
- German
- Italian
- Serbian
- Ukrainian

67

♥ ROSA SALVA HOTEL

- Calle Fiubera San Marco 951, 30124 Venice Italy
- 009 39 041 241 3323

Property amenities

- Free High Speed Internet (WiFi)
- Complimentary Instant Coffee
- Children's television networks
- Taxi service
- 24-hour security
- Baggage storage
- 24-hour front desk

- Express check-in / check-out
- Wifi
- Complimentary tea
- Special diet menus
- Concierge
- Non-smoking hotel
- Private check-in / check-out

Room features

- Allergy-free room
- Soundproof rooms
- Air conditioning
- Safe
- Telephone
- Minibar
- Flatscreen TV
- Walk-in shower
- VIP room facilities

- Laptop safe
- Wake-up service / alarm clock
- Refrigerator
- Bath / shower
- Complimentary toiletries
- Hair dryer

Room types

- City view
- Non-smoking rooms
- Suites

LANGUAGES SPOKEN

- English
- French
- Spanish
- German
- Italian

♥ HOTEL SATURNIA & INTERNATIONAL VENEZIA
● Via XXII Marzo, San Marco 2398, 30124 Venice Italy

Property amenities

- Free High Speed Internet (WiFi)
- Free breakfast
- Babysitting
- Highchairs available
- Pets Allowed (Dog / Pet Friendly)
- Airport Transportation
- Business Center with Internet Access
- Banquet room
- Wifi
- Bar / lounge
- Restaurant
- Breakfast available
- Breakfast buffet
- Breakfast in the room
- Kid-friendly buffet
- Special diet menus
- Taxi service
- Meeting rooms
- Spa
- Steam room
- Rooftop terrace
- 24-hour security
- Baggage storage
- Concierge
- Currency exchange
- Non-smoking hotel
- Sun loungers / beach chairs
- Sun terrace
- Doorperson
- First aid kit
- 24-hour check-in
- 24-hour front desk
- Private check-in / check-out
- Dry cleaning
- Laundry service
- Ironing service

Room features

- Blackout curtains
- Air conditioning
- Housekeeping
- Interconnected rooms available
- Private balcony
- Minibar
- Flatscreen TV
- Bidet
- Room service
- Safe
- Telephone
- Laptop safe
- Private bathrooms
- Wake-up service / alarm clock
- Refrigerator

- Bath / shower
- Complimentary toiletries
- Hair dryer

Room types

- Non-smoking rooms
- Suites
- Family rooms

LANGUAGES SPOKEN

- English
- French
- Spanish
- German
- Italian

♥ RUZZINI PALACE HOTEL

- Castello 5866, 30122 Venice Italy
- 009 39 041 241 0447

Property amenities

- Free High Speed Internet (WiFi)
- Bar / lounge
- Babysitting
- Airport Transportation
- 24-hour security
- Baggage storage
- 24-hour front desk
- Private check-in / check-out
- Wifi
- Breakfast available
- Complimentary tea
- Special diet menus

- Taxi service
- Concierge
- Non-smoking hotel
- Shared lounge / TV area
- Doorperson
- First aid kit
- Umbrella
- Shoeshine

Room features

- Blackout curtains
- Soundproof rooms
- Air conditioning
- Desk
- Coffee / tea maker
- Flatscreen TV
- Extra-long beds
- Bath / shower
- Private balcony
- Room service
- Safe
- Sofa
- Telephone
- VIP room facilities
- Clothes rack
- Laptop safe
- Wake-up service / alarm clock
- Minibar
- Electric kettle
- Sofa bed
- Complimentary toiletries
- Hair dryer

Room types

- Landmark view
- Bridal suite
- Non-smoking rooms
- Suites

♥ ALBERGO MARIN

- Ramo delle Chioverete Sestiere Santa Croce 670/b, 30135 Venice Italy
- 009 39 041 852 1532

Property amenities

- Free High Speed Internet (WiFi)
- Free breakfast
- Children's television networks
- Highchairs available
- Taxi service
- 24-hour security
- Baggage storage
- 24-hour check-in
- Wifi
- Bar / lounge
- Coffee shop

- Breakfast available
- Breakfast buffet
- Complimentary tea
- Kid-friendly buffet
- Special diet menus
- Non-smoking hotel
- Doorperson
- First aid kit
- 24-hour front desk
- Express check-in / check-out

Room features

- Air conditioning
- Housekeeping
- Safe
- Telephone
- Coffee / tea maker
- Electric kettle
- Cable / satellite TV
- Bidet

- Wardrobe / closet
- Iron
- Private bathrooms
- Wake-up service / alarm clock
- Flatscreen TV
- Walk-in shower
- Bath / shower
- Complimentary toiletries
- Hair dryer

Room types

- Non-smoking rooms

LANGUAGES SPOKEN

- English
- French
- Spanish
- German
- Italian

FUN ACTIVITIES: BE AN ADVENTURER

Scavenger Hunt: Venice's Hidden Gems

Welcome, young explorers, to the magical maze of Venice, a city filled with secrets waiting to be uncovered. Are you ready for an adventure like no other? Grab your explorer's hat and join us on a scavenger hunt to discover Venice's hidden gems. With each clue solved and every challenge met, you'll see Venice through the eyes of a true adventurer. Let's explore our quest to find hidden treasures in this city of dreams.

Clue 1: The Guardian Lions

- **Your Quest:** Find the ancient guardians of Venice, the proud lions sculpted in stone.
- **Hint:** These majestic creatures stand watch by the entrance of a place where books are treasured as much as gold.
- **Reward:** Snap a photo with these silent sentinels and discover the name of the square they call home.

Clue 2: Marco Polo's Home

- **Your Quest:** Seek out the house of Venice's famous explorer, Marco Polo. Though the original home no longer stands, a plaque marks where his tales of distant lands began.
- **Hint:** Wander the maze of streets in the Castello district to find this marker of history.
- **Reward:** Imagine the tales Marco Polo could tell and jot down an adventure you'd like to embark on in your explorer's journal.

Clue 3: The Whispering Gallery

- **Your Quest:** Find the spot where whispers travel across stone and secrets can be shared from afar.
- **Hint:** This architectural marvel is nestled within the palace where Venice's rulers once walked.
- **Reward:** Share a secret with a fellow adventurer across the gallery and marvel at the magic of sound.

Clue 4: The Bookshop of Wonders

- **Your Quest:** Discover a bookshop where books and gondolas meet, and stories float on the water.
- **Hint:** Seek this treasure in the heart of Venice, where books find their home in bathtubs and boats.
- **Reward:** Choose a postcard that captures the spirit of your adventure and send it to a friend, or keep it as a souvenir.

Clue 5: The Bridge with No Parapets

- **Your Quest:** Cross the bridge that offers no support, where Venetians once tested their balance and bravery.
- **Hint:** This unique bridge can be found in the sestiere of Cannaregio, spanning a narrow canal.
- **Reward:** Carefully cross to the other side and earn the title of "Braveheart of Venice."

Clue 6: The Hidden Vineyard

- **Your Quest:** In a city of water, seek out the rare sight of a Venetian vineyard tucked away from the bustling canals.
- **Hint:** This green oasis lies hidden behind high walls in the Dorsoduro district, a reminder of Venice's connection to the earth.

- **Reward:** Peek through the gates and dream of the flavours that these grapes will bring to life.

Clue 7: The Secret Bakery

- **Your Quest:** Follow your nose early in the morning to find the bakery where sweet treats are prepared before sunrise.
- **Hint:** Hidden in one of Venice's narrow alleys, this bakery doesn't have a sign, but the smell of fresh pastries will guide you.
- **Reward:** Choose a delicious pastry as your prize, a taste of Venice to fuel the rest of your adventure.

Congratulation! You've uncovered the hidden gems of Venice, each stop on your scavenger hunt revealing a new layer of this enchanting city. With every clue solved and challenge met, you've seen Venice as tourists and true adventurers. Keep your explorer's spirit alive, for every city, town, and place you visit has secrets waiting to be discovered. Who knows where your next adventure will take you?

ACTIVITIES AND JOURNAL: REMEMBERING YOUR JOURNEY

Welcome, young adventurers, to a creative way to remember your magical journey through Venice. A Venetian diary isn't just any diary; it's a treasure chest of memories filled with sketches, stories, and souvenirs from your voyage through this enchanting city. Let's explore how you can create a diary that captures the essence of Venice, making your memories last a lifetime.

START WITH A SKETCH

- **Canals and Gondolas:** Sit by a canal and sketch the gondolas as they glide. Don't worry about perfecting it; it's all about capturing the moment.

- **Architectural Wonders:** Try drawing the intricate facade of St. Mark's Basilica or the sweeping arches of the Rialto

Bridge. These architectural details will bring your diary to life.

WRITE YOUR STORIES

- **A Day as a Venetian:** Imagine you're a Venetian kid living in this water-filled city. Write a story about your day, from morning until night. What adventures would you have?

_____
_____
_____
_____
_____
_____
_____

- **The Mystery of the Mask:** Venice is famous for its masks. Write a short story about finding a mysterious mask that leads you on an unexpected adventure.

_____
_____
_____
_____
_____
_____
_____

COLLECT SOUVENIRS

- **Tickets and Tokens:** Keep your vaporetto tickets, museum passes, or other tokens from your journey. They're perfect for pasting into your diary.

- **Pressed Flowers or Leaves:** If you visit a garden or find a beautiful plant in Venice, carefully press a leaf or flower between the pages of your diary as a natural souvenir.

FUN FACTS AND QUIZ: TEST YOUR VENICE KNOWLEDGE

Now that you've explored Venice and filled your diary with memories, it's time to test your knowledge with fun facts and a quick quiz. Can you answer these questions about Venice?

FUN FACTS

- ♥ Venice is made up of over 100 tiny islands connected by more than 400 bridges.
- ♥ The Venetian Republic was one of Europe's most powerful economic and military forces for centuries.
- ♥ Venice has no cars; boats are the primary mode of transportation.

QUIZ

1. **What is the main square in Venice called?** A) Piazza San Marco B) Piazza Venezia C) Piazza Roma

2. **What is the name of the famous bridge that crosses the Grand Canal?** A) Ponte Vecchio B) Ponte di Rialto C) Ponte dei Sospiri

3. **What is a traditional Venetian boat called?** A) Canoe B) Gondola C) Kayak

4. **What festival is Venice famous for, where people wear elaborate masks and costumes?** A) Carnevale B) Festival di Venezia C) La Biennale

Answers

1) Piazza San Marco

2) Ponte di Rialto

3) Gondola

4) Carnevale

Creating your Venetian diary is a journey in itself, a way to keep the magic of Venice alive long after you've returned home. Through sketches, stories, and souvenirs, you've captured memories that will tell the story of your adventure for years to come. And with each fun fact and quiz question, you've become a visitor and a true explorer of Venice's rich history and vibrant culture. Keep exploring, keep dreaming, and remember—every page of your diary is a new adventure waiting to happen.

FAREWELL TO VENICE

As the sun sets over the lagoon, casting a golden glow over the city of canals, it's time to say, "Arrivederci, Venezia." Our journey through this enchanting city has been filled with adventure, discovery, and magic only Venice can offer. From the grandeur of St. Mark's Basilica to the serene beauty of its hidden canals, Venice has shared its stories, its history, and its heart with us.

❖ REFLECTIONS ON THE WATER

As you reflect on your time in Venice, remember the moments that took your breath away—the first glimpse of the Rialto Bridge, the gentle sound of water lapping against the gondolas, and the laughter of children chasing pigeons in Piazza San Marco. These memories are now a part of your story, treasures that you'll carry with you long after you've left Venice's shores.

❖ LESSONS LEARNED

Venice has taught us the importance of curiosity and the joy of discovery. We've learned to navigate the city's maze of canals and the journey of exploring new places and cultures. We've seen the value of preserving history and the environment, ensuring that the beauty of Venice can be enjoyed by generations to come.

❖ KEEPING THE MAGIC ALIVE

Even as we say goodbye, the magic of Venice doesn't have to end. You can keep it alive by sharing your stories and memories with others. Create art inspired by your adventures, cook a Venetian meal for your family, or tell the tales of the city to anyone willing to listen. Each time you do, you'll be transported back to those narrow streets and sparkling waters.

❖ A PROMISE TO RETURN

Venice, with its timeless beauty and endless mysteries, has a way of calling us back. So, as we bid farewell, let it not be a goodbye but a promise to return. Venice will be waiting, ready to reveal new secrets and new adventures.

As the pages of our Venetian diary close, we look back with gratitude for our shared journey. Venice, a city of dreams and stories, has left its mark on our hearts. And though we may depart, the call of Venice—its beauty, history, and spirit—will stay with us, always inviting us to return to its welcoming waters.

Arrivederci, Venezia. Until we meet again, keep your canals glistening, your gondolas gliding, and your stories unfolding. Our adventure may be over for now, but the memories and the magic of Venice will forever be a part of us.

VENICE WORD SEARCH

Q	B	C	V	X	D	X	V	M	V	N	Y	J	O	R	P	M	O	Q	W	I	C
G	E	C	Q	R	B	E	N	E	Y	O	M	M	L	H	A	A	V	Y	O	U	N
V	Q	R	N	T	B	Q	I	A	T	E	S	N	U	S	A	D	K	E	W	K	U
N	C	S	U	N	P	V	I	O	E	N	L	Q	K	B	G	D	T	A	I	P	S
M	R	W	T	I	D	S	D	Y	D	X	G	S	L	E	D	G	K	O	R	G	N
G	N	I	K	G	L	S	P	B	R	L	V	K	G	M	L	V	C	O	O	C	Y
G	M	W	F	R	T	G	G	M	S	I	R	C	N	F	K	G	E	D	M	M	Q
K	O	B	R	G	O	A	Q	M	V	A	U	K	B	B	T	V	H	L	H	P	W
V	E	R	T	N	P	U	J	X	W	H	C	F	A	V	V	B	R	L	F	X	L
P	P	D	D	G	V	H	Q	V	J	I	F	H	G	R	C	H	E	C	B	J	J
N	O	O	M	X	N	S	D	K	T	W	A	E	R	H	F	X	X	S	L	B	F
T	L	A	S	B	D	W	L	S	F	N	C	N	L	Y	J	E	S	A	X	P	P
A	C	U	I	T	S	A	J	A	S	L	G	T	H	F	V	F	D	H	S	X	B
Y	E	Y	G	K	L	J	H	E	N	M	T	W	G	J	G	T	J	H	H	A	C
N	K	H	P	O	O	V	X	S	O	A	B	B	X	J	A	T	E	S	O	U	T
M	U	R	A	N	O	W	D	W	P	W	C	H	A	O	X	H	S	U	B	O	T
J	S	K	V	G	S	I	G	L	N	U	Y	S	Q	C	S	H	B	R	U	X	B
V	F	J	J	C	W	J	M	J	X	X	X	Y	A	U	Q	D	K	A	R	I	D
N	U	W	W	U	G	M	S	S	Y	D	J	O	T	L	A	I	R	Q	A	J	U
W	K	Q	V	L	U	G	R	J	H	K	I	H	P	W	T	U	S	W	U	C	D
M	P	A	W	R	H	E	X	W	S	L	H	L	M	A	S	B	O	Q	F	R	F
U	N	E	R	U	P	E	L	J	B	T	N	G	U	Y	F	M	V	F	Q	S	Y

Canals   Masks   Rialto

Gondola   Murano

VENICE WORD SEARCH

M	M	Y	R	Y	J	J	Q	A	J	N	P	V	Q	O	L	N	M	Q	C	H	K
B	H	C	J	M	G	L	P	G	U	V	X	I	L	B	V	F	D	C	C	W	P
F	C	R	Q	J	R	M	N	D	P	W	S	E	U	P	A	H	J	J	O	R	R
L	X	L	V	V	C	T	U	N	P	V	J	I	F	H	F	O	K	U	A	W	T
S	C	C	M	A	E	J	H	O	P	Y	J	F	J	D	T	S	Q	Q	J	F	J
M	J	R	X	Q	Y	A	U	Q	W	W	T	E	V	T	E	P	A	H	D	J	H
Y	Y	L	E	S	P	V	D	M	V	H	J	W	E	D	G	I	X	H	R	W	O
M	P	H	M	O	V	S	T	X	J	A	O	R	I	R	O	U	X	C	P	Y	V
P	O	Q	J	G	D	K	R	Q	R	N	O	H	W	J	D	Q	G	E	O	I	M
H	V	L	D	B	S	L	X	X	F	P	J	O	O	V	G	O	B	D	J	V	U
K	T	A	L	W	I	M	P	H	A	M	O	I	S	Z	M	K	V	G	U	V	L
O	X	V	U	J	Y	P	P	V	I	K	V	L	P	X	Z	K	D	E	Y	T	P
U	J	I	S	K	B	O	Y	T	P	P	N	F	X	R	E	A	K	V	V	C	M
U	N	N	I	V	B	A	S	I	L	I	C	A	I	B	Q	A	L	R	V	H	M
P	M	R	S	N	N	Y	S	W	U	S	A	B	K	N	X	T	I	A	X	V	V
N	Q	A	C	R	U	D	K	D	K	M	G	V	I	J	F	Q	A	B	P	F	S
O	U	C	A	E	K	W	J	W	B	B	I	R	A	M	O	B	H	M	D	M	E
P	S	Y	U	L	K	S	A	K	X	V	H	X	M	G	P	A	V	A	N	D	B
B	T	V	A	W	B	J	P	I	J	L	M	I	N	O	K	V	F	H	K	R	T
T	R	J	J	V	O	C	A	Y	N	P	Y	K	M	Y	M	L	B	K	U	G	R
P	S	K	P	R	Y	C	V	T	G	W	L	F	O	R	U	X	M	C	Y	S	K
N	Y	V	R	T	A	A	H	U	P	L	R	Y	O	G	Q	E	N	I	E	E	C

Basilica   Doge   Vaporetto
Carnival   Palazzo

VENICE WORD SEARCH

I	V	F	C	V	U	W	I	F	C	Q	X	Q	R	M	N	D	I	W	L	E	U
I	S	G	C	A	N	U	G	A	L	C	A	R	K	W	Q	E	I	O	O	F	H
S	U	B	O	N	D	M	K	V	A	F	B	S	X	S	T	W	X	C	A	Q	F
G	P	S	V	S	G	C	P	T	T	S	O	A	W	T	I	I	B	J	E	F	T
G	H	D	O	X	A	A	D	R	M	A	M	R	V	C	V	H	U	A	R	Y	P
R	K	G	L	Y	E	M	T	D	U	M	Y	K	P	L	D	C	D	K	U	O	M
R	P	W	Q	H	K	P	G	K	X	I	N	R	L	E	G	L	H	L	T	S	S
T	U	W	L	X	Y	A	N	Y	J	S	K	N	U	W	E	C	M	M	Y	S	Y
D	D	J	M	C	H	N	J	V	C	S	B	X	A	L	V	H	M	I	H	G	O
O	L	M	K	P	M	I	U	U	L	I	H	K	O	C	L	C	U	T	P	I	L
E	I	J	W	P	Q	L	L	G	U	N	A	O	E	V	M	A	E	Y	N	N	S
G	D	V	P	P	V	E	T	A	H	E	J	Y	E	G	M	A	X	U	W	O	A
D	L	O	T	A	L	E	G	J	F	R	W	V	E	E	I	J	G	L	C	K	K
I	T	Q	A	E	R	H	X	R	J	E	F	Q	N	K	Y	F	X	S	T	O	D
R	J	X	G	X	V	J	M	B	O	S	O	N	F	X	Q	K	Q	U	U	U	L
B	N	Y	U	H	B	S	I	R	J	N	Y	E	A	X	W	Y	Y	J	D	B	Y
W	F	F	I	R	B	R	F	U	S	M	E	A	S	I	L	B	A	S	T	O	J
X	E	L	H	S	J	E	H	O	J	K	I	R	R	F	Q	X	C	U	B	S	B
M	H	N	T	S	P	R	J	U	F	K	A	Q	W	Y	Y	D	W	U	G	W	L
F	O	Y	U	R	F	O	S	L	E	G	L	H	E	M	T	M	T	V	P	F	D
L	B	L	V	W	A	H	J	J	B	L	L	Q	Q	E	C	B	O	R	B	G	O
U	B	G	V	Y	P	U	F	E	H	X	W	F	M	J	D	I	M	D	L	F	V

Bridge Gelato Serenissima
Campanile Laguna

88

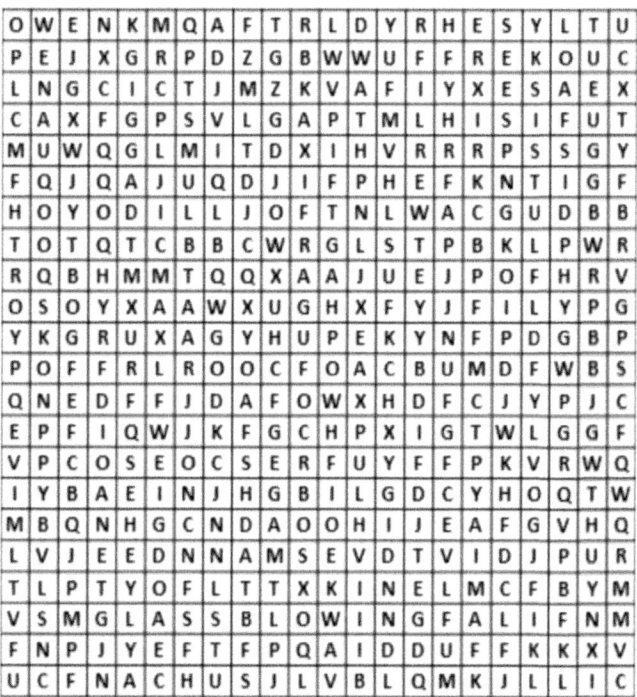

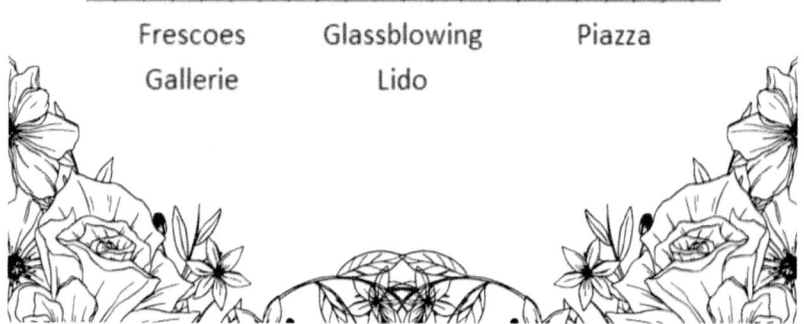

VENICE WORD SEARCH

O	W	E	N	K	M	Q	A	F	T	R	L	D	Y	R	H	E	S	Y	L	T	U
P	E	J	X	G	R	P	D	Z	G	B	W	W	U	F	F	R	E	K	O	U	C
L	N	G	C	I	C	T	J	M	Z	K	V	A	F	I	Y	X	E	S	A	E	X
C	A	X	F	G	P	S	V	L	G	A	P	T	M	L	H	I	S	I	F	U	T
M	U	W	Q	G	L	M	I	T	D	X	I	H	V	R	R	R	P	S	S	G	Y
F	Q	J	Q	A	J	U	Q	D	J	I	F	P	H	E	F	K	N	T	I	G	F
H	O	Y	O	D	I	L	L	J	O	F	T	N	L	W	A	C	G	U	D	B	B
T	O	T	Q	T	C	B	B	C	W	R	G	L	S	T	P	B	K	L	P	W	R
R	Q	B	H	M	M	T	Q	Q	X	A	A	J	U	E	J	P	O	F	H	R	V
O	S	O	Y	X	A	A	W	X	U	G	H	X	F	Y	J	F	I	L	Y	P	G
Y	K	G	R	U	X	A	G	Y	H	U	P	E	K	Y	N	F	P	D	G	B	P
P	O	F	F	R	L	R	O	O	C	F	O	A	C	B	U	M	D	F	W	B	S
Q	N	E	D	F	F	J	D	A	F	O	W	X	H	D	F	C	J	Y	P	J	C
E	P	F	I	Q	W	J	K	F	G	C	H	P	X	I	G	T	W	L	G	G	F
V	P	C	O	S	E	O	C	S	E	R	F	U	Y	F	F	P	K	V	R	W	Q
I	Y	B	A	E	I	N	J	H	G	B	I	L	G	D	C	Y	H	O	Q	T	W
M	B	Q	N	H	G	C	N	D	A	O	O	H	I	J	E	A	F	G	V	H	Q
L	V	J	E	E	D	N	N	A	M	S	E	V	D	T	V	I	D	J	P	U	R
T	L	P	T	Y	O	F	L	T	T	X	K	I	N	E	L	M	C	F	B	Y	M
V	S	M	G	L	A	S	S	B	L	O	W	I	N	G	F	A	L	I	F	N	M
F	N	P	J	Y	E	F	T	F	P	Q	A	I	D	D	U	F	F	K	K	X	V
U	C	F	N	A	C	H	U	S	J	L	V	B	L	Q	M	K	J	L	L	I	C

Frescoes Glassblowing Piazza
Gallerie Lido

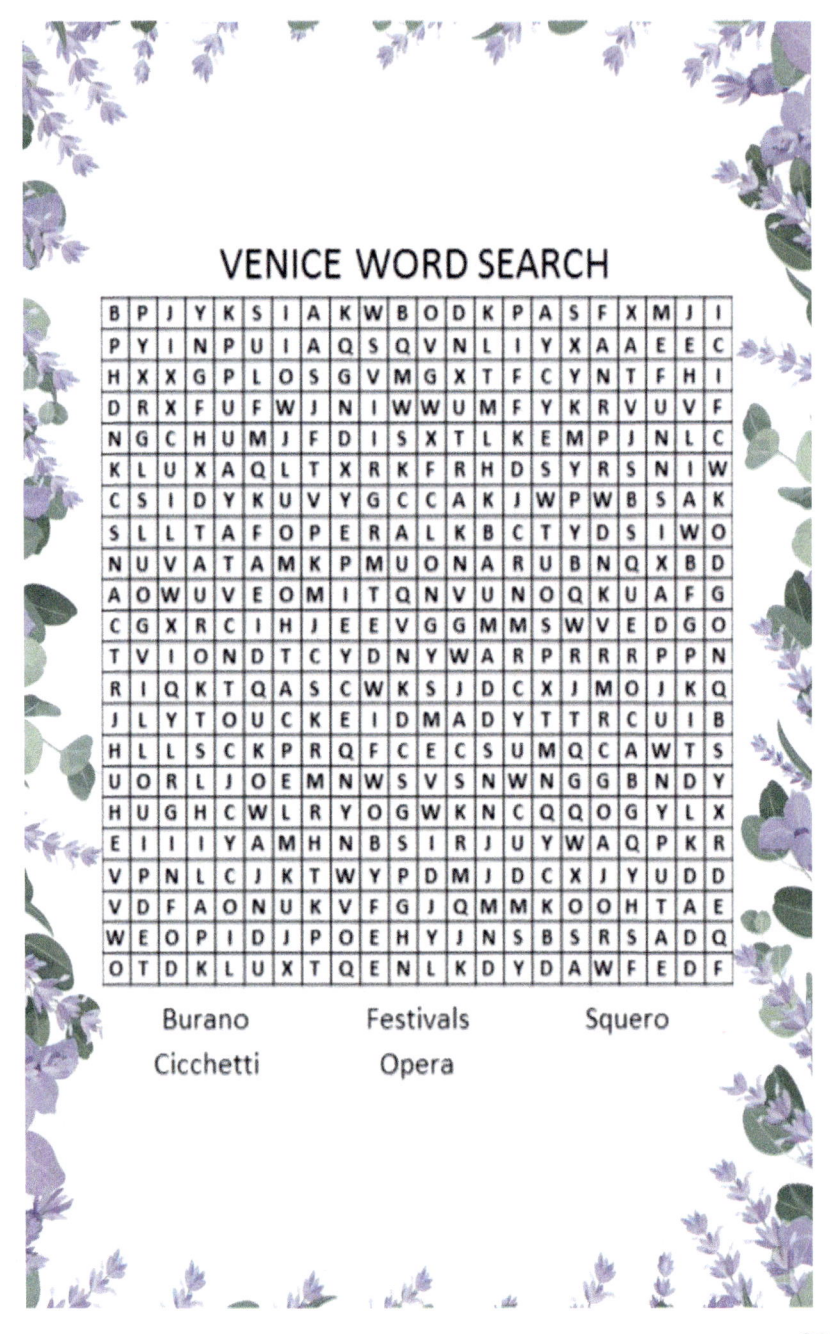

VENICE WORD SEARCH

B	P	J	Y	K	S	I	A	K	W	B	O	D	K	P	A	S	F	X	M	J	I
P	Y	I	N	P	U	I	A	Q	S	Q	V	N	L	I	Y	X	A	A	E	E	C
H	X	X	G	P	L	O	S	G	V	M	G	X	T	F	C	Y	N	T	F	H	I
D	R	X	F	U	F	W	J	N	I	W	W	U	M	F	Y	K	R	V	U	V	F
N	G	C	H	U	M	J	F	D	I	S	X	T	L	K	E	M	P	J	N	L	C
K	L	U	X	A	Q	L	T	X	R	K	F	R	H	D	S	Y	R	S	N	I	W
C	S	I	D	Y	K	U	V	Y	G	C	C	A	K	J	W	P	W	B	S	A	K
S	L	L	T	A	F	O	P	E	R	A	L	K	B	C	T	Y	D	S	I	W	O
N	U	V	A	T	A	M	K	P	M	U	O	N	A	R	U	B	N	Q	X	B	D
A	O	W	U	V	E	O	M	I	T	Q	N	V	U	N	O	Q	K	U	A	F	G
C	G	X	R	C	I	H	J	E	E	V	G	G	M	M	S	W	V	E	D	G	O
T	V	I	O	N	D	T	C	Y	D	N	Y	W	A	R	P	R	R	R	P	P	N
R	I	Q	K	T	Q	A	S	C	W	K	S	J	D	C	X	J	M	O	J	K	Q
J	L	Y	T	O	U	C	K	E	I	D	M	A	D	Y	T	T	R	C	U	I	B
H	L	L	S	C	K	P	R	Q	F	C	E	C	S	U	M	Q	C	A	W	T	S
U	O	R	L	J	O	E	M	N	W	S	V	S	N	W	N	G	G	B	N	D	Y
H	U	G	H	C	W	L	R	Y	O	G	W	K	N	C	Q	Q	O	G	Y	L	X
E	I	I	I	Y	A	M	H	N	B	S	I	R	J	U	Y	W	A	Q	P	K	R
V	P	N	L	C	J	K	T	W	Y	P	D	M	J	D	C	X	J	Y	U	D	D
V	D	F	A	O	N	U	K	V	F	G	J	Q	M	M	K	O	O	H	T	A	E
W	E	O	P	I	D	J	P	O	E	H	Y	J	N	S	B	S	R	S	A	D	Q
O	T	D	K	L	U	X	T	Q	E	N	L	K	D	Y	D	A	W	F	E	D	F

Burano   Festivals   Squero

Cicchetti   Opera

VENICE WORD SEARCH

B	E	L	H	H	X	I	I	U	N	U	L	K	R	U	J	O	Q	W	D	C	R
U	L	J	T	S	O	F	E	M	N	K	E	C	G	W	F	Y	I	Q	S	Q	K
T	D	W	O	K	V	Y	V	W	W	P	Q	E	F	U	A	H	Q	B	L	F	I
W	L	L	J	T	N	Y	S	Y	W	V	D	G	U	A	C	B	H	A	P	X	P
U	F	E	S	K	P	R	K	O	I	G	E	U	C	D	M	I	L	C	P	X	O
I	T	O	H	W	T	C	I	N	O	Q	K	Y	A	F	M	O	A	W	K	N	C
Q	Q	O	Y	R	E	Q	W	C	B	B	K	G	N	M	Y	T	A	M	F	B	W
O	S	W	C	X	V	U	I	J	M	G	E	R	C	U	S	A	B	E	H	J	G
N	V	T	N	F	B	S	I	F	G	G	Y	I	A	C	T	V	L	Q	K	A	K
B	V	R	A	U	U	S	D	V	J	U	C	T	G	Y	F	R	P	K	V	K	W
D	U	L	N	F	J	M	S	B	R	Q	S	T	Y	V	J	H	O	L	C	K	K
T	W	M	J	W	G	K	W	O	K	O	L	I	I	P	P	I	J	F	E	O	Y
N	S	T	J	U	E	Y	C	J	E	X	O	S	R	X	Q	X	U	N	B	T	E
M	R	T	A	Y	E	U	W	A	H	F	P	O	Q	I	H	B	C	Y	S	T	W
C	L	T	N	W	S	V	S	T	G	P	G	Y	R	M	X	U	R	S	S	E	R
S	H	U	J	O	W	L	E	S	H	T	X	L	A	A	A	R	C	U	H	R	B
H	F	E	E	H	P	C	D	E	D	J	B	Q	S	R	T	O	A	X	T	O	L
K	L	F	J	D	B	Y	O	F	P	Q	A	V	Y	V	J	T	S	J	C	T	N
J	B	Q	N	V	V	H	I	K	X	M	R	A	B	S	J	W	A	A	I	N	V
W	B	L	E	K	W	D	H	G	H	Q	L	X	S	X	L	D	T	G	O	I	G
K	O	T	P	H	Y	A	T	X	K	I	G	W	W	X	B	W	G	P	E	T	W
F	D	W	O	J	U	E	B	J	O	B	C	W	K	Y	L	F	U	G	P	R	D

Festa   Gritti   Tintoretto

Fortuny   Regatta

VENICE WORD SEARCH

B	E	L	H	H	X	I	I	U	N	U	L	K	R	U	J	O	Q	W	D	C	R
U	L	J	T	S	O	F	E	M	N	K	E	C	G	W	F	Y	I	Q	S	Q	K
T	D	W	O	K	V	Y	V	W	W	P	Q	E	F	U	A	H	Q	B	L	F	I
W	L	L	J	T	N	Y	S	Y	W	V	D	G	U	A	C	B	H	A	P	X	P
U	F	E	S	K	P	R	K	O	I	G	E	U	C	D	M	I	L	C	P	X	O
I	T	O	H	W	T	C	I	N	O	Q	K	Y	A	F	M	O	A	W	K	N	C
Q	Q	O	Y	R	E	Q	W	C	B	B	K	G	N	M	Y	T	A	M	F	B	W
O	S	W	C	X	V	U	I	J	M	G	E	R	C	U	S	A	B	E	H	J	G
N	V	T	N	F	B	S	I	F	G	G	Y	I	A	C	T	V	L	Q	K	A	K
B	V	R	A	U	U	S	D	V	J	U	C	T	G	Y	F	R	P	K	V	K	W
D	U	L	N	F	J	M	S	B	R	Q	S	T	Y	V	J	H	O	L	C	K	K
T	W	M	J	W	G	K	W	O	K	O	L	I	I	I	P	P	I	J	F	E	O	Y
N	S	T	J	U	E	Y	C	J	E	X	O	S	R	X	Q	X	U	N	B	T	E
M	R	T	A	Y	E	U	W	A	H	F	P	O	Q	I	H	B	C	Y	S	T	W
C	L	T	N	W	S	V	S	T	G	P	G	Y	R	M	X	U	R	S	S	E	R
S	H	U	J	O	W	L	E	S	H	T	X	L	A	A	A	R	C	U	H	R	B
H	F	E	E	H	P	C	D	E	D	J	B	Q	S	R	T	O	A	X	T	O	L
K	L	F	J	D	B	Y	O	F	P	Q	A	V	Y	V	J	T	S	J	C	T	N
J	B	Q	N	V	V	H	I	K	X	M	R	A	B	S	J	W	A	A	I	N	V
W	B	L	E	K	W	D	H	G	H	Q	L	X	S	X	L	D	T	G	O	I	G
K	O	T	P	H	Y	A	T	X	K	I	G	W	W	X	B	W	G	P	E	T	W
F	D	W	O	J	U	E	B	J	O	B	C	W	K	Y	L	F	U	G	P	R	D

Festa   Gritti   Tintoretto
Fortuny   Regatta

VENICE WORD SEARCH

X	P	U	R	E	S	K	J	E	E	I	C	S	X	N	O	J	R	U	K	A	N
D	T	N	G	B	G	C	Y	H	G	S	T	O	P	E	D	E	T	X	N	I	L
S	O	H	Y	P	P	V	H	O	L	L	R	U	D	I	K	J	W	U	L	G	R
V	H	L	B	R	Q	S	S	P	J	H	M	C	D	X	G	D	Y	V	J	S	I
C	N	C	N	K	G	I	H	A	B	O	J	X	W	F	N	F	O	C	F	T	B
I	G	Q	D	P	I	I	F	X	X	B	J	O	Q	P	D	N	K	M	W	C	M
L	G	X	P	K	E	H	B	S	W	A	G	H	O	X	N	Q	N	B	K	B	T
F	B	M	C	R	A	Y	L	M	N	L	B	Q	V	W	F	W	G	T	W	L	S
A	R	C	U	N	A	M	S	W	W	O	P	A	B	N	I	O	B	M	C	L	V
A	E	A	D	Y	W	P	J	K	O	U	B	F	D	T	U	V	X	B	D	T	H
E	Q	H	R	E	I	N	E	V	A	C	S	O	A	I	F	N	M	F	G	B	O
E	S	P	Q	Y	K	N	H	R	Y	S	N	N	L	I	O	B	G	N	R	K	Q
B	C	E	H	D	I	O	E	L	A	N	E	S	R	A	N	D	Y	Q	U	X	E
S	K	C	N	E	E	H	U	S	Q	H	O	I	R	N	J	H	U	D	T	N	Y
U	Y	U	K	O	S	L	L	M	A	U	J	I	P	F	J	S	N	Q	X	S	S
D	N	N	S	M	R	S	J	J	P	S	B	G	B	H	N	M	C	E	P	M	X
V	Y	J	B	V	V	E	L	F	D	B	R	G	T	D	Y	C	R	M	U	F	X
Q	F	W	T	J	K	R	V	D	K	Y	M	B	H	H	W	O	Y	F	I	W	L
L	J	M	G	L	L	R	I	H	O	K	A	F	H	A	M	X	T	P	H	L	P
O	K	B	A	C	O	S	S	Q	O	X	Y	A	P	M	I	F	S	U	R	E	W
S	E	M	P	R	X	J	K	Y	A	O	N	U	W	H	F	L	O	D	K	K	P
S	M	Y	E	K	O	N	O	Q	S	F	A	G	S	E	T	V	N	R	V	T	Q

Arsenale   Scuola   Veronese

Ca'   Venier

VENICE WORD SEARCH

Q	P	B	T	T	W	X	K	F	E	K	C	S	O	B	L	Q	T	S	I	F	X
Y	A	W	J	N	S	C	K	W	G	P	F	T	C	P	R	P	P	B	W	B	X
N	C	U	N	O	J	W	S	X	Y	H	T	S	A	V	W	A	A	V	V	G	W
W	V	O	O	M	S	S	V	E	D	E	F	R	I	Q	P	F	B	L	W	A	Y
U	F	E	M	G	D	W	N	S	H	I	Q	K	V	M	J	L	I	V	F	O	I
B	V	H	E	T	U	C	T	G	U	C	W	L	O	Q	X	A	R	C	I	S	G
O	O	F	P	P	U	O	A	U	L	K	Y	U	L	D	B	D	D	P	H	Q	S
K	O	Y	Q	M	W	R	V	W	K	H	B	X	C	V	Y	G	H	Q	M	P	F
T	C	S	M	E	T	S	E	N	Q	Y	X	K	I	E	Y	T	I	N	O	W	I
Y	M	P	W	L	L	J	M	Y	L	W	W	B	C	B	T	E	M	R	M	L	P
Y	Q	G	B	S	X	U	S	G	D	M	L	A	A	K	W	U	S	D	K	E	L
N	Q	M	D	Q	Y	W	J	E	B	W	I	X	N	V	O	H	O	D	S	X	M
L	L	B	L	O	J	M	T	P	S	I	H	D	D	W	C	I	G	C	Y	F	O
K	V	K	Q	D	U	K	N	X	C	T	G	L	T	K	J	K	H	L	I	U	S
Q	N	O	J	S	O	K	H	U	E	U	I	N	F	B	Y	E	V	L	T	A	L
M	B	U	J	P	P	X	J	M	N	K	R	E	M	G	R	W	H	A	G	Y	Y
D	U	V	R	A	F	H	G	F	E	B	V	A	R	I	E	I	N	C	T	S	N
N	K	E	U	A	Q	X	K	T	Q	M	J	W	A	I	G	P	J	B	W	I	E
X	U	O	U	N	O	V	J	X	D	E	M	X	I	U	X	M	T	T	R	C	T
O	T	N	T	Q	Q	Q	T	U	H	C	B	O	Y	P	Q	I	G	R	P	L	N
V	U	V	J	M	G	E	C	L	M	T	V	S	U	L	Y	I	R	L	D	R	O
E	T	P	R	X	J	K	F	S	B	G	U	V	H	R	F	H	V	D	D	U	P

Ciclovia   Ponte   Traghetto
Pescheria   Sestieri

VENICE WORD SEARCH

A	T	L	G	L	B	Q	F	F	Q	R	G	B	V	U	V	K	O	A	Y	S	V
D	R	L	P	M	M	S	E	L	A	V	E	N	R	A	C	E	K	I	I	T	B
E	F	K	F	E	K	J	S	U	F	J	N	S	I	R	Q	S	S	R	W	C	A
X	U	V	Q	S	V	K	H	O	W	O	H	Y	U	S	P	L	T	E	M	X	S
G	B	I	O	O	E	O	R	M	J	P	L	L	V	G	F	L	X	C	E	U	T
B	E	F	K	G	S	R	Q	G	C	M	Q	C	S	P	Y	F	A	C	S	P	J
H	M	V	D	Q	A	V	Y	O	D	F	C	O	H	V	H	D	A	I	C	B	M
O	I	V	L	J	R	A	R	U	I	L	S	H	H	X	I	C	N	T	H	H	E
W	E	G	P	N	P	H	B	M	C	E	P	S	E	V	R	C	B	S	C	V	S
M	D	O	O	R	Y	A	D	Y	B	X	F	O	X	Q	C	X	D	A	S	O	P
P	U	Z	U	P	D	L	R	X	H	L	C	I	L	A	O	H	F	P	P	I	O
T	A	Z	E	D	W	H	C	N	I	O	C	M	C	E	V	T	X	V	S	J	I
O	P	A	S	F	W	U	E	S	M	O	L	N	D	K	T	K	D	V	Q	V	E
B	J	R	I	B	V	J	E	S	X	V	R	H	L	C	P	S	S	O	O	M	J
C	O	R	B	H	F	W	X	H	E	I	N	J	I	O	N	V	R	J	N	R	W
F	P	E	O	P	P	M	A	N	Q	C	L	T	G	P	S	H	F	L	U	R	L
W	R	T	P	M	I	Q	E	I	R	A	C	A	B	J	V	W	Q	L	T	R	S
H	M	V	J	M	T	T	P	I	S	D	C	I	U	B	R	Q	X	T	D	B	C
I	I	G	P	Y	I	C	A	E	C	R	B	A	U	U	L	F	V	B	Q	Y	L
U	K	T	J	A	Q	A	J	J	U	J	U	K	N	I	O	B	C	P	D	R	Q
X	G	R	N	U	B	E	R	A	S	Q	B	T	A	S	S	Q	P	P	L	T	Y
B	S	Y	R	H	J	T	X	C	A	V	G	F	A	T	W	K	I	G	P	W	X

Bacari Pasticceria Venetian
Carnevale Terrazzo

VENICE WORD SEARCH (Solution)

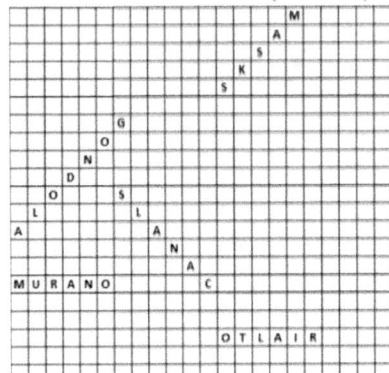

VENICE WORD SEARCH (Solution)

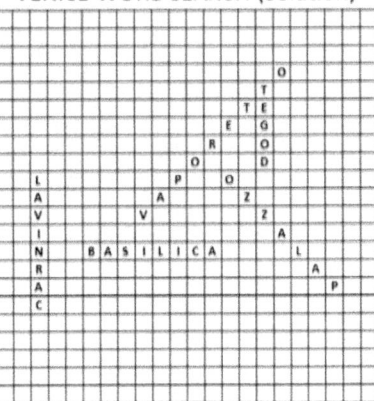

VENICE WORD SEARCH (Solution)

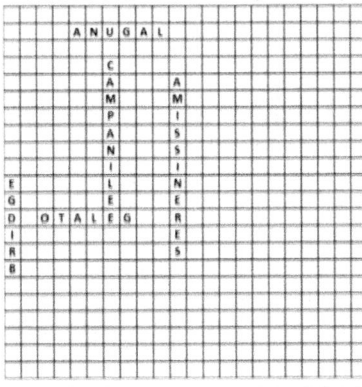

VENICE WORD SEARCH (Solution)

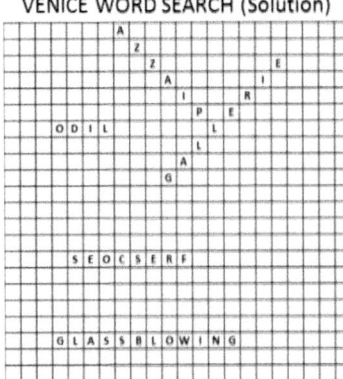

VENICE WORD SEARCH (Solution)

96

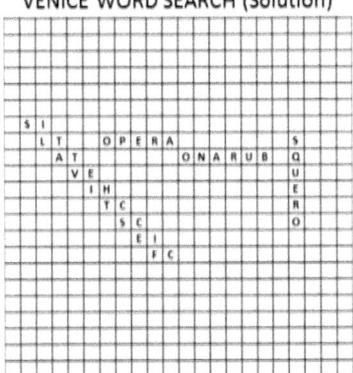

VENICE WORD SEARCH (Solution)

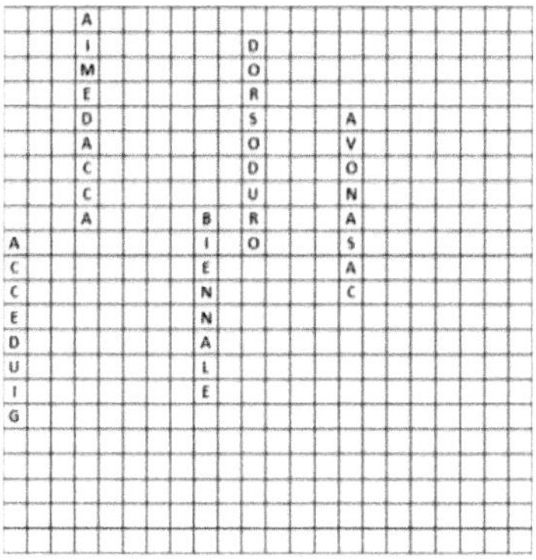

VENICE WORD SEARCH (Solution)

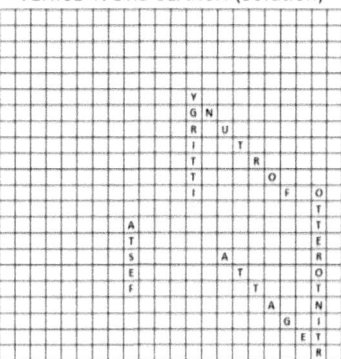

VENICE WORD SEARCH (Solution)

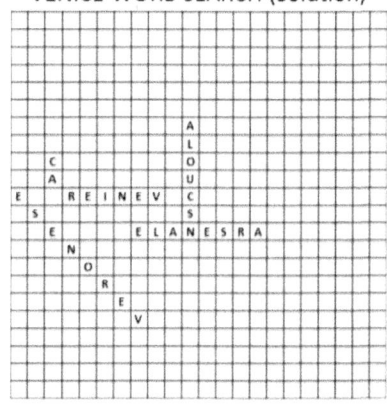

VENICE WORD SEARCH (Solution)

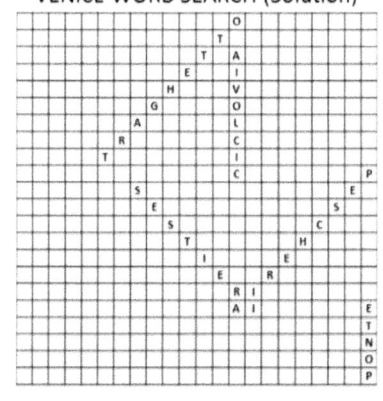

VENICE WORD SEARCH (Solution)

97

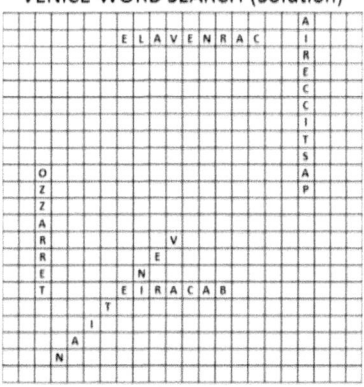

Printed in Great Britain
by Amazon